Economic Sanctions as Instruments of American Foreign Policy

Economic Sanctions as Instruments of American Foreign Policy

Zachary Selden

PRAEGER

Westport, Connecticut
London

Library of Congress Cataloging-in-Publication Data

Selden, Zachary A.
    Economic sanctions as instruments of American foreign policy /
Zachary Selden.
        p.   cm.
    Includes bibliographical references (p.   ) and index.
    ISBN 0–275–96387–X (alk. paper)
        1. Economic sanctions, American.   2. United States—Foreign
relations.   I. Title.
    JZ6373.S45   1999
    327.1'17—dc21   98–38288

British Library Cataloguing in Publication Data is available.

Library of Congress Catalog Card Number: 98–38288
ISBN: 0–275–96387–X

First published in 1999

Praeger Publishers, 88 Post Road West, Westport, CT 06881
An imprint of Greenwood Publishing Group, Inc.
www.praeger.com

Printed in the United States of America

The paper used in this book complies with the
Permanent Paper Standard issued by the National
Information Standards Organization (Z39.48–1984).

10 9 8 7 6 5 4 3 2 1

Contents

Figures and Tables

FIGURE

TABLE

Introduction

The United States occupies a unique place in the international environment. Regardless of the extent to which the U. S. turns to multilateral security arrangements, it is still the only state capable of projecting significant military power anywhere in the world. Its security assurances are vital to maintaining peace, or at least stability, in many regions.

For a variety of practical and political reasons, the United States cannot respond to every crisis with military force. But ignoring ethnic slaughter or the proliferation of sophisticated weapons technology, for example, only begs for further trouble. The complexity of the post-Cold War environment has driven policymakers to turn to options between military force and inaction. Economic sanctions fit in between these poles, and have become virtually the default option in American foreign policy.

Since the fall of the Berlin Wall, the U. S. has used sanctions dozens of times to address everything from nuclear proliferation to human rights concerns. This explosion of sanctions has led to a larger debate over their utility. On one side, pundits deride all sanctions as useless without stopping to consider the forms they might take and the subtleties with which they can be imposed. On the other, Congress has seen fit to impose a blizzard of generally ineffective sanctions, and some promote sanctions as virtually an alternative to military force.

The truth about sanctions is somewhat more nuanced than the debate suggests. Economic sanctions are often worse than ineffective; in many cases, they have altered the target country's economy and internal politics in ways that have made that state's offensive behavior even more difficult to reverse. At the same time, sanctions have been successful in many instances.

The key to the effective use of sanctions is understanding how and why they produce such divergent effects. Economic sanctions have a place in the foreign policy tool kit, and will continued to be employed. Sanctions cannot replace military force, but they can have very real effects on the economy of the targeted state. Economic pain, however, does not always translate into political change. Sanctions can create trade distortions that economically benefit groups of producers and suppliers within the target country. In doing so they can create a constituency with a vested interest in seeing that sanctions, and the policies that prompted them, remain in place.

This book aims to be a guide to the more effective use of sanctions. It would not have been possible without grants from the Center for International and Strategic Affairs at UCLA, as well as International Studies and Overseas Programs. I have benefited from comments and critiques from numerous individuals. Chief among them is Richard Rosecrance, but I would also like to thank the staff at the British Public Records Office and the British Library of Economics and Political Science for their assistance, Michael Szporluk for his invaluable assistance in helping me navigate life during wartime in Beograd, Evan Osborne and Charles Wharton for statistical help, Amie Kreppel for being there and keeping me sane, and most of all my parents, Irving and Renee.

1

Economic Sanctions in American Foreign Policy

Great powers enjoy a range of options when deciding how to respond to events that threaten their security. At one end of the continuum there is military force, at the other, inaction. The post-Cold War environment, however, exacerbates the pitfalls of these two extremes. Without a clear adversary, the United States, as have other great powers in history, runs the risk of assuming the role of global policeman, becoming embroiled in conflicts that cannot be resolved quickly, and do not serve core American security interests. Inaction taken to its extreme is isolationism, which is fraught with dangers of its own. While there is no single power capable of threatening the United States currently, it is possible, and indeed probable, that one will arise if the United States significantly retreats from world affairs. Therefore, the options that fall in between these poles take on added importance in the current global environment.

The end of the Cold War and the accompanying clarity of mission it lent to American foreign policy means military intervention is now more difficult to justify. First, there is the overriding question of when the use of force can be justified with regard to its costs. Without any challenger on the horizon, it is highly unclear what constitutes a threat to U. S. security that needs to be addressed with military force together with its inherent sacrifices in life and expenditure. Second, what should be the criteria for intervention? At the same time that American forces were attempting to restore order to Somalia in 1992, there were several other similar conflicts in progress on the African continent. Liberia was also in turmoil, but, rather than send in troops, the U. S. removed all its nonessential embassy staff and allowed the various factions to continue to fight. Perhaps it was the more extensive media coverage of the misery in Somalia that prompted American action, or the relative closeness of Somalia to the Diego Garcia military installation, but it seems the height of ad hoc policy-making to allow the media or sheer convenience to determine what is a significant enough threat to U. S. interests to require military intervention.

In addition to these questions, there is the basic problem that all conflicts that arise are not necessarily suited to military intervention. The Somalia intervention is considered a failure not because of the initial deployment, but because once basic order was restored the military was placed in an inappropriate role. A victim of "mission creep," the Somalia intervention ended with the ignominious retreat of American forces.

Despite these problems and questions, there have been notably successful uses of military force in recent years such as the Gulf War, Panama, and the Haiti intervention. In brief strikes using overwhelming force (or in the case of Haiti, the dispatch of military force that was received peaceably), the United States quickly achieved its goals with minimal casualties. While these are important cases, all of these interventions featured fortuitous circumstances that tilted the odds in favor of success. The Gulf War was fought on flat, open terrain where air power could achieve spectacular results. Panama was home to one of the largest garrisons of American forces in the Western hemisphere. It is an invitation to disaster to assume that all such situations will be as easily resolved.

But the case for the use of military force presupposes that an interventionist role for the United States is desirable. Observers from all ends of the political spectrum have argued for the United States to reduce its international military commitments and focus on domestic issues. With the Cold War fought and won, the threats to American security are said to be of a different nature. On the international level, economic competitiveness is key, and the U. S. has sacrificed its economic interests to maintain harmonious relations with its allies at its own peril. Addressing the security concerns of the twenty-first century requires that we turn our attention inward and confront the social maladies that plague American society and ultimately threaten American economic competitiveness.

Isolationism, however, is a dangerous alternative because small threats can become large ones. If, for example, the United States had chosen to ignore Saddam Hussein's attempts at regional hegemony and Israel had chosen to ignore his atomic weapons program, we might currently be faced with a nuclear-armed Iraq in control of one-fifth of the world's oil supply. Inaction on the part of a great power has historically led to greater challenges. Britain allowed its fleet to dwindle after its battles with revolutionary France only to face a larger threat just a few years later in the form of Napoleon. A hundred years later, British inaction allowed Hitler to grow from a relatively minor problem into what was arguably Britain's fiercest challenge. While the temptation to ignore potential threats is high, inaction is a historically dangerous option.

If inaction and military forms of intervention have serious drawbacks, then the intermediary options become all the more important. Economic sanctions are one option that has become increasingly popular in recent years. Most countries are dependent on foreign goods in at least some crucial areas of their economy, and this international interdependence can be exploited to register displeasure with the actions of a particular country. By restricting the flow of certain goods and services to the country in question, it will suffer some deprivation and be forced to change its ways in order to rejoin the community of nations and the economic benefits therein. Because economic rather than military strength is increasingly seen by many as the prime determinant of international power, sanctions may begin to assume an even more prominent role.[1]

Sanctions against Haiti, Yugoslavia, Libya, and Iraq are the most familiar recent examples, but the United States used sanctions 25 times during the 1980s alone to influence the actions of other states. In the post-Cold War era, sanctions have become virtually the default option in American foreign policy, and are imposed to correct everything from human rights violations to nuclear proliferation. While they are a popular tool of foreign policy, little is known as to how and why sanctions are effective or ineffective. We often hear that sanctions "never work" or that they only "need a little more time" to take effect, but what are the critical variables that determine the success or failure of sanctions? Why is it that sanctions often seem to produce exactly the opposite behavior from what was expected and desired? As sanctions become an increasingly used tool in the foreign policy kit, it is critical that we answer these questions in a systematic manner. Otherwise we are more likely to pull out a wrench when a hammer would be more effective, and vice versa. This study provides a guide to the effective use of economic pressure, and in doing so, expands and refines the repertoire available to policy makers.

THE DIFFERING EFFECTS OF FINANCIAL, IMPORT, AND EXPORT SANCTIONS

Any discussion of economic sanctions requires disaggregating the different types of sanctions and their effects. Sanctions can either block financial transactions or block trade. Within the latter category, a further distinction must be made between sanctions which block the flow of goods to a state (export sanctions) and sanctions that block the flow of goods from a state (import sanctions). This is a critical distinction because sanctions that stop or slow the flow of goods to a country can function as a protective tariff for those producers capable of supplying substitutes. On the other hand, sanctions that prevent a country from selling its products in the world marketplace should not have any such benefits. In this manner, import sanctions should be more effective than export sanctions because the connection between economic pain and political change is not diluted by unintentional benefits to producers.

Most economic studies of export sanctions conclude that they generally do not impose a serious economic burden on the country, which is why they fail to cause the desired political changes. Substitutes and alternative sources of supply are often readily available on the world market, and a single country rarely has the requisite control over the supply of a particular good to unilaterally impose a significant embargo.[2] In addition, as Johan Galtung has pointed out, the target will gradually become adjusted to sanctions, thus diminishing their effect.[3] Yet there are many instances in which export sanctions did impose a significant economic burden on the economy, but still failed to have the desired political effect. This presents a paradox that cannot be resolved by conventional economic explanations. However, if we consider the ramifications of the fact that export sanctions often function as a protective tariff and induce import substitution industrialization (ISI), there is an alternative explanation. Producers and alternate suppliers of the embargoed goods will benefit from this protection and take action in the political arena to ensure that their protective shield remains in place, which may help to explain why countries whose trade is distorted by economic sanctions often respond with a nationalist backlash.

This "Rally Around the Flag" effect is based on the idea that sanctions provide a common external enemy to unite the population of the target country and increase the popularity of the current leadership. While this can be seen as a psychological phenomenon, the rally effect has an economic basis as well. Export sanctions tend to create groups of economic gainers who have a material incentive to see that sanctions are maintained and, who may influence the target country government to maintain the policies that prompted sanctions.

Rhodesia, which experienced stringent sanctions throughout the 1960s, is a classic example of the perverse effect sanctions can have on an economic, and in turn, political system. Because of the ban on traditional Rhodesian exports, especially tobacco, it was expected that sanctions would lead to high unemployment and unrest among the white population of Rhodesia. But this did not happen because the new import substitution industries absorbed most of the excess labor. Between 1965 and 1975, manufacturing output in Rhodesia rose by 88%, and the range of output expanded from 602 products in 1963 to 3,837 in 1970 with six of the nine fastest growing industries in infrastructure, especially chemicals, petroleum products, and construction.[4]

Contemporary observers found that, "The imposition of rigid import controls, especially on consumer goods, necessitated by the fall in exports, has led to considerable import substitution. New firms have begun and old ones have expanded."[5] Rhodesia was subjected to some of the most stringent sanctions in history and, while there were some notable problems in maintaining the requisite international cooperation to keep sanctions in place, the Rhodesian experience provides a clear example of the powerful inducements to produce provided by sanctions.

All of this flies in the face of the conventional wisdom surrounding sanctions. When sanctions were first imposed by the British government in 1965, British officials were highly confident that their strategy would bring the Rhodesian government to its knees. In early 1966, British Prime Minister Harold Wilson stated that sanctions would bring the Smith government of Rhodesia down "within weeks."[6] Minister of Commonwealth Affairs Earnest Bowden asserted a year later that, "Given a little time--and it is not very much more than six weeks--I think you will be quite happy with the results of selective mandatory sanctions."[7] Even *The Economist* abandoned its usually restrained tone to declare that stringent sanctions "would undoubtedly be enough to bring the Rhodesian economy to a virtual halt within a few months."[8] These predictions turned out to be utterly wrong. The Smith government did not collapse within weeks or months. It took until 1979, a full 14 years, until the Rhodesian government agreed to a negotiated settlement incorporating black majority rule.

The unintended consequence of sanctions in this case was to create a protected market for domestic producers of import substitutes. Sanctions are not protection per se, but rather a functional equivalent.[9] Any one of a number of exogenous factors can either cheapen or make international trade more expensive, thereby either helping or harming owners and users of relatively scarce factors.[10] We focus here on economic sanctions because while other exogenous changes may affect the gains (and losses) from trade, sanctions are now a standard tool in the repertoire of foreign policy professionals. Sanctions are imposed, unlike many other exogenous factors such as transport costs that are altered by technological advancement and, as such, the debate surrounding their imposition in particular cases should be much more informed by a systematic study of their unintended effects.

The rally effect is one possible response to sanctions, but the desired response would be the "Fifth Column" effect. This is centered on the idea that sanctions will harm the interests of some sectors in the target country, who will in turn exert pressure on their government to comply with the demands of the sender. While economic theory predicts that groups that own or intensively use scarce factors will benefit from protection, it also holds that groups that own or use factors in which the country is relatively well endowed will lose from increased protection or exogenous changes that function as a form of protection. Therefore, if export sanctions create groups of gainers who benefit from sanctions, they also harm the interests of groups that rely on imports or export-oriented producers, if the sanctions restrict the ability of the target country to export.

On the other hand, gainers from sanctions will constitute an interest group that has every incentive to see that sanctions, and the policies that prompted them, stay in place. In addition, the groups that gain from sanctions also will be gaining financial resources, which they should rationally be willing to expend some proportion of in the pursuit of their interests. Conversely, the groups that lose from sanctions will find themselves in a financially diminished position, which may reduce their political influence.

ECONOMIC SANCTIONS IN HISTORICAL PERSPECTIVE

Economic sanctions have been employed in various forms since Pericles issued the Megarian Decree during the Peloponnesian War, and scholars have been writing on the topic for nearly as long.[11] To begin with the obvious, if we are to determine if economic sanctions are effective or counterproductive, it is necessary to determine why they are imposed. The basic assumption is that the imposition of economic pain will force the target to behave in a manner consistent with the sender's preferences. Sanctions are therefore aimed at either changing the particular offensive policies or removing the leaders responsible for them.[12] Yet, sanctions also fill a part of the gray area on the continuum between diplomacy and war. They are often used when the transgression being addressed is not enough to justify the use of force, when the use of force is politically impossible, or when the sender country or organization needs to demonstrate its resolve. We also cannot ignore the important role domestic politics in the sender country can play in deciding when, and against whom, to impose sanctions.

Even a cursory perusal of the historical record reveals that sanctions are usually imposed when pure diplomacy has failed and overt warfare is simply out of the question. For example, the United States was not going to risk a nuclear conflagration over the Soviet invasion of Afghanistan. Sanctions were imposed as a means of demonstrating the United States' resolve. This point is important because as game theoretic models show, indicating resolve can alter the preferences of the opposing party.[13] In this manner at least, economic sanctions can have some real effect on international bargaining.

Domestic political pressures often drive the imposition of sanctions. British Prime Minister David Lloyd George is reported to have said that the 1935 League of Nations sanctions against Italy, "came too late to save Abyssinia, but just in the nick of time to save the (British) Government."[14] This may be an extreme case, but clearly the imposition of sanctions can have distinct political rewards in the sender nation. The sanctions imposed by the United States on the Republic of South Africa can be viewed in this light. The Reagan Administration, preferring to continue with a policy of "constructive engagement," had no desire to impose the sanctions but was compelled to do so in order to quell congressional and other domestic voices that called for the sanctions. While such domestic concerns are not the entirety of the story, they definitely have an impact on the sender country's decision to impose sanctions.

The increased use of sanctions after World War II gave birth to a considerable body of research. While many express reservations about their effectiveness, Hufbauer and Schott find that sanctions are most effective when there are close relations between the imposing (sender) and receiving (target) countries and when the sender's demands are minor.[15] However, according to Lisa Martin, David Baldwin, and others, the critical variable in determining success is the degree of international cooperation achieved in imposing sanctions.[16] The greater the international cooperation, the greater the probability of imposing an unacceptable cost on the target country, thus forcing it to alter its behavior in a manner consistent with the interests of the sender. None of the previous studies of sanctions, however, sufficiently differentiates between the various types of sanctions. While import and financial sanctions should become more effective as international cooperation increases, the counterproductive elements associated with export sanctions should increase with international cooperation.

Other scholars have noted that sanctions may induce unanticipated behavior in some targets. Thomas Willett concludes that, "The increased cost to the target government of continuing its policies seldom outweighs the political cost of appearing to give in to foreign influences. Sanctions may not only make it more difficult politically for the target government to modify their behavior, but may even induce more aggressive or restrictive behavior."[17] Willett's speculation is quite probably correct, but this leads to the question of what types of sanctions are most likely to induce this sort of behavior.

Many economists have examined the theoretical possibilities that sanctions could have unanticipated side-effects that benefit particular sectors of the economy.[18] J. H. Cooper in particular argues that sanctions may stimulate domestic production and benefit capital intensive industries in general.[19] While it is clear that several economists and scholars from other disciplines have noted the import substitution effects of sanctions, none has tried to examine this effect over a sample of cases and how it varies depending on the type of sanction.

In general, the literature on sanctions tends to fall into two categories: extended case studies that note the industrial substitution process in one country but make no attempt to generalize these observations and theoretical economic discussions lacking in empirical data. Some have noted that sanctions seem to have promoted industrial development in specific cases.[20] At the same time, others have discussed the possible unanticipated effects of sanctions.[21] Yet even the most comprehensive work on sanctions to date, Hufbauer and Schott's *Economic Sanctions Reconsidered*, does not fully take into account the counterproductive effects of export sanctions.

One final point must be addressed regarding the utility of economic sanctions: the critical element of time. Individuals and states adapt rapidly to changing economic incentives, and the oil crisis of the 1970s provides a clear illustration of this behavior. When the first oil shocks hit the United States in the early 1970s, some predicted that the price of oil would skyrocket and remain high well into the foreseeable future. But this was not to be the case. In response to higher prices, individuals cut down on oil consumption, use of alternative fuels increased, industry became more efficient in its use of petroleum-based products, and auto manufacturers began to produce more fuel-efficient cars.

The European reaction to the 1973 oil crisis was even more spectacular. An investigation of European Economic Community records revealed that, "There was at no time a real shortage of petroleum on the European market. Consumption simply responded to the increase in prices."[22] In other words, Europe adapted so quickly to what was expected to be crippling sanctions that there was never any real net effect. It is true that individuals were forced to alter their behavior, but the embargo failed to cause significant damage to the European economy. Sanctions force the price of certain goods up, thereby encouraging conservation, substitution and domestic production. It is difficult to determine how long this process of adaptation will take, but as the preceding examples demonstrate, it is a certainty that it does take place.

This point pertains to the events leading up to the Gulf War. When the U. S. Congress was debating whether or not to grant the President authorization to use armed force to eject the Iraqi army from Kuwait, the argument was often heard that, "sanctions had not been given enough time to work."[23] While it is true that the import sanctions that prevented Iraq from selling its oil were crippling and would become increasingly so over time, the efficacy of export sanctions may be eroded over time because of the ability of individuals to adapt to economic changes. Therefore, past a certain point, to give this type of sanction more time to work may simply be to give it more time to fail conclusively.

Export sanctions have consequences beyond their intended effects. The Committee on Economic Sanctions noted in 1932 that, "we must also reckon with the possible effect of the consciousness that a blockade might invoke in stimulating military preparedness... now more than ever important to ordnance, ammunition factories and raw materials within one's own frontiers."[24] The effects of the blockade of Germany during World War I were not entirely lost on the Committee, but their work apparently did nothing to dissuade the League of Nations from imposing sanctions against Italy only three years later.

This does not mean that sanctions and economic statecraft should be entirely abandoned. Sanctions that block the flow of capital to a target country, or restrict its ability to export, can be highly effective. No matter what the economic effects of a particular sanctions episode actually are, they do have their place in signaling resolve. The world economy is more interrelated today than ever before, and this interdependence can be exploited in a variety of ways. But economic sanctions have limits and possible unintended consequences that any policymaker should be aware of before employing them.

While particular sanctions episodes have been subject to intense scrutiny, the effects of different types of sanctions have not been considered in a systematic manner. Chapter 2 quantifies the import substitution effects, and then demonstrates the political ramifications of this process in several cases, including South Africa. Chapters 3, 4, and 5 conduct three detailed case studies. The first focuses on the American embargo of Great Britain 1807-11, the second examines the use of sanctions against Yugoslavia in the 1990s, and the third examines the use of sanctions against Iraq before the Gulf War. Chapter 6 unites the case studies with the theoretical framework and sets out an agenda for further research on how states can, and cannot, use their economic power to affect the behavior of other states.

NOTES

1. Richard Rosecrance, *The Rise of the Trading State* (New York: Basic Books, 1986).

2. See, for example, Per Lundborg, *The Economics of Export Embargoes: The Case of U. S.-Soviet Grain Suspension* (London: Croom-Helm, 1987), Richard Porter, "International Trade and Investment Sanctions: Potential Impact on the South African Economy," *Journal of Conflict Resolution,* 23, no. 4 (1979): 579-612, T. Willett and M. Jalaighajar, "U. S. Trade Policy and National Security," *Cato Journal,* 3, no. 3 (1983): 717-28.

3. Johan Galtung, "On The Effect of International Economic Sanctions," *World Politics,* 19, no. 3 (1967): 378-416.

4. Harry Strack, *Rhodesia: The Case of Sanctions* (Lincoln: University of Nebraska Press, 1976), 90.

5. R.B. Sutcliffe, "The Political Economy of Economic Sanctions," *Journal of Commonwealth Studies,* 7, no. 2 (1969) : 114.

6. Douglas Anglin, "United Nations Economic Sanctions Against Rhodesia and South Africa," in *The Utility of Economic Sanctions,* ed. David Leyton-Brown (London: Croom-Helm, 1985), 1.

7. Muriel Grieve, *"Economic Sanctions: Theory and Practice,"* *International Relations* 3, no. 1 (October 1968): 435.

8. Economist Intelligence Unit, *Quarterly Economic Review of Rhodesia, Zambia and Malawi,* 52 (December 1965): 2.

9. This is based on the Stolper-Samuelson theorem which states that trade protection will benefit groups who own or intensively use factors of production with which, relative to the rest of the world, the country is poorly endowed. W.F. Stolper and P. Samuelson, "Protection and Real Wages," *Review of Economic Studies,* 9, no. 1, (1941): 58-73.

10. Ronald Rogowski, *Commerce and Coalitions: How Trade Affects Domestic Political Alignments* (Princeton: Princeton University Press, 1989).

11. Stephanie Ann Lenway notes that both Baldwin and Hufbauer and Schott use the Megarian Decree as a starting point but draw different lessons. For Hufbauer and Schott the Decree helped to make war between Athens and Sparta inevitable. Baldwin , however sees the Decree as a final attempt to avoid war and the prudent step for Athens to take before initiating hostilities against

Sparta and its allies. Stephanie Ann Lenway, "Between War and Commerce: Economic Sanctions as a Tool of Statecraft," *International Organization*, 42, no. 2 (Spring 1988).

12. M. Nincic and P. Wallensteen, "Economic Coercion and Foreign Policy," in *Dilemmas of Economic Coercion: Sanctions in World Politics*, eds. M. Nincic and P. Wallensteen (New York: Praeger Publishers, 1983): 4.

13. See, for example, G. Snyder and P. Diesing, *Conflict Among Nations* (Princeton: Princeton University Press, 1977).

14. Peter Rowland, *David Lloyd George: A Biography* (New York: Macmillan Press, 1975): 723.

15. Gary Hufbauer, J. Schott, and K. Elliott, *Economic Sanctions Reconsidered* (Washington DC: Institute for International Economics, 1985):49.

16. David Baldwin, *Economic Statecraft* (Princeton: Princeton University Press, 1985); Lisa Martin, *Coercive Cooperation* (Princeton: Princeton University Press, 1991); M. Doxey, *Economic Sanctions and Problems of International Enforcement* (London: Oxford University Press, 1971); W. Kaempfer and A. Lowenberg, *International Economic Sanctions* (Boulder: Westview Press, 1992); Klaus Knorr, "Economic Interdependence and National Security," in *Economic Issues and National Security*, eds. Klaus Knorr and F. Trager (Lawrence: University of Kansas Press, 1982); Nincic and Wallensteen, "Economic Coercion and Foreign Policy"; Richard Porter, "International Trade and Investment Sanctions," *Journal of Conflict Resolution* 23, no. 4 (1979):579-612; George Tsebelis, "Are Sanctions Effective?: A Game Theoretic Analysis," *Journal of Conflict Resolution* 34, no. 1 (1990): 3-28.

17. Willett and Jalaighajar, "U. S. Trade Policy and National Security."

18. For example see J. H. Cooper, "Sanctions and Economic Theory," *South African Journal of Economics* 53, no. 3 (1985): 287-96; B. E. Dollery, "Apartheid and the Case for Sanctions," *Journal of Commonwealth and Comparative Politics* 26, no. 3 (1988): 338-40; J. M. Linsay, "Trade Sanctions as Policy Instruments: A Re-examination," *International Studies Quarterly* 30, no. 2 (1986): 153-74.

19. J. H. Cooper, "On Income Distribution and Economic Sanctions," *South African Journal of Economics* 57, no. 1 (1989): 14-21.

20. Robin Renwick, *Economic Sanctions* (Cambridge: Harvard University Center for International Affairs, 1981).

21. W. Kaempher and A. Lowenberg, "The Theory of International Economic Sanctions: A Public Choice Approach," *The American Economic Review*, 78 (September 1988); Knorr, "Economic Interdependence and National Security"; Nincic and Wallensteen, "Economic Coercion and Foreign Policy"; Tsebelis, "Are Sanctions Effective?"

22. R. Prodi and A. Clo, "Europe," in *The Oil Crisis* , ed. Raymond Vernon (New York: Norton Press, 1976): 101.

23. See, for example, U. S. House of Representatives Committee on Armed Services, *The Role of Sanctions in Securing U. S. Interests in the Persian Gulf* (Washington D.C., December 21, 1990): 11; Gary Hufbauer and Kimberly Elliott, "Sanctions Will Bite and Soon," *New York Times*, 14 January 1991: A17.

24. Evans Clark, ed., *Boycotts and Peace. A Report by the Commission on Economic Sanctions* (New York: Harper and Row, 1932).

2

Disaggregating the Effects of Economic Sanctions

The three basic types of sanctions (financial, export, and import) should have very different effects. If export sanctions promote import substitution, import sanctions and financial sanctions should not.[1] More important, however, are the political consequences. Because export sanctions function as a protective tariff benefiting producers of import substitutes, these producers have a strong incentive to see that sanctions, and the policies that prompted them, remain in place.

These effects are not peculiar to the postwar era. In fact historical examples of the unintended developmental side effects of sanctions abound. The "Continental System" of Napoleonic Europe was essentially the equivalent of strict import sanctions. Beginning in 1807, Napoleon attempted to completely close off continental Europe to English exports. The purpose was twofold: to develop continental industry by reducing dependence on imports and to bring England to ruin by destroying the commercial trade on which it relied. Napoleon succeeded in developing continental industry but failed in ruining the financial stability of England.[2]

Napoleon used import sanctions because he was following the mercantilist suppositions of his time, which dictated that trade was an essentially predatory activity. Napoleon was quite willing to sell to the English if they were willing to buy. Since Britain's strategy was guided by the same conception of trade, the focus of its economic warfare was to deny entry to goods from French-controlled Europe.

Two fortuitous events aided the French and nearly forced Britain to compromise with Napoleon. First, because of British actions against neutral shipping, the American government imposed export sanctions between 1807 and 1811, which seriously reduced British grain imports. Second, nature conspired to compound the effects of the American sanctions. The year 1810 was a disastrous harvest year in Britain, which drove it to negotiate a compromise solution with the United States. Incredibly, Napoleon came to the aid of the British and allowed them to purchase European grain. Once again he was operating on the mercantilist assumption that trade is a predatory activity with the importer on the losing end of the transaction.

Before exploring the reasons for the mixed results of Napoleon's policy, it is necessary to address the fact that these were self-imposed sanctions. It makes no difference if the sanctions are imposed from the outside or, as in this case, are self-imposed, because the results will be the same. The price of the embargoed goods is forced up, consumers lose but that loss is mitigated by gains to domestic producers. In this case, Napoleon believed the gain was strategic enough to counterbalance whatever losses were experienced. It makes no difference if the blockade orders are written in French or English, the fundamental laws of economics still apply.

Although Napoleon was able to develop continental industry and increase France's self-sufficiency, he was not able to economically strangle England. British commerce continued to flow, albeit through neutral channels to the continent, and the British expanded their trade with the New World and the colonies. The end result was that not only did the English economy fail to collapse as predicted by the French, but the English government generated greater revenue from duties imposed on the increasing trade with which to fund the war effort.[3]

The experience of Nazi Germany provides a more modern example of the same situation. In August 1936, Hitler produced the Four Year Plan designed to commit Germany to an autarchic form of self-sufficiency. The object was to make Germany as invulnerable as possible to the sort of blockade that Hitler correctly envisioned would be imposed on Germany on the commencement of hostilities. [4] The Four Year Plan did not differ tremendously from Napoleon's "Continental System" in its primary goal and methods: It was another case of self-imposed sanctions designed to produce exactly the sort of self-sufficiency that enabled Germany to wage an aggressive war for nearly six years. Germany was able to produce synthetic oil and rubber to fuel the war effort in the absence of imports, and munitions production more than doubled between 1942 and 1944. In fact, munitions production did not begin to decline until the last quarter of 1944.[5] Once again, it would have made little difference if these sanctions had been imposed from without rather than from within.

We can model the import substitution effects of export sanctions with the following example. Let us assume that country X has embarked on a policy that many nations find abhorrent, and in order to force country X to change its ways, the United Nations imposes economic sanctions aimed at cutting off the flow of arms and strategic items. Let us assume that these are stringent sanctions and there are no "sanctions-busters," that is, none of the participants in the sanctions effort will violate the agreement.

The imposition of export sanctions ostensibly reduces the supply of the goods in question to zero and, while this is an unattainable goal, it can be assumed that the supply will certainly decrease. Therefore, the price will go up, creating an incentive for domestic production of the embargoed goods, provided the country has the technical ability to do so.

In this manner, sanctions can become the functional equivalent of a protective tariff by screening out foreign-produced goods and stimulating domestic production. In the long run, sanctions can actually aid in the development of domestic industries capable of satisfying national needs, reducing the target's economic interdependence with the rest of the world and, in turn, the ability of other nations or international organizations to influence the target's behavior through economic channels. Therefore, not only can the imposition of sanctions fail to produce the desired short-term effects, they may also have serious long-term consequences.

Figure 2.1 is essentially a model of tariff-distorted production in which Pf is the price at free trade, Ps is the price under sanctions, and s represents the reduced supply under sanctions. H' is the quantity produced domestically under free trade and H'' is the quantity produced domestically under sanctions. M' is the quantity imported under sanctions and M'' is the quantity imported under free trade.

As sanctions reduce the flow of imports, they force up the price of those goods and the demand for domestic substitutes. This effect is graphically represented by the areas (a b c) and (d e f) where (a b c) is the amount by which domestic production must increase to offset the decrease in imports shown in area (d e f). Therefore the potential increase in profits to domestic producers of formerly imported products screened out by sanctions is the product of the difference between supply before and after sanctions, and the difference between the volume of imports before and after sanctions (Ps-Pf)*(M'-M''). Actual profit would be the product of the difference between supply before and after sanctions, and the difference between the volume of domestically produced substitutes before and after sanctions (Ps-Pf)*(H"-H').

Figure 2.1
Welfare Loss to Consumers and Producer Gain under Sanctions

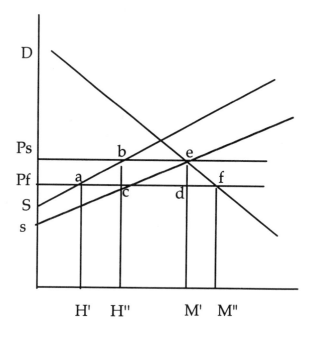

This operates on the unrealistic assumption that demand will remain constant, that is, it is completely inelastic. Domestic substitutes will be more expensive than imports; if this were not the case, then the country in question would not have imported the goods under free trade conditions. While demand will decrease with increased prices, it most likely will not completely evaporate. Therefore, depending on the elasticity of demand of the goods blocked by sanctions, the demand curve may shift downwards but the model will retain its validity. The size of the areas (a b c) and (d e f) will shrink but will not disappear unless demand is perfectly elastic.

While export sanctions may be generally ineffective and in many cases counterproductive, there are several variables that will positively affect the utility of economic sanctions. First there is the elasticity of demand in the target country to consider, but the level of development of the target country and the availability of substitutes or alternate suppliers for the sanctioned goods may also be critical. Export sanctions aimed at products with relatively inelastic demand functions should meet with greater success than sanctions aimed at products with more elastic demand. This of course assumes that the senders are able to control the supply of the goods in question so that alternate suppliers do not simply step in to fill the gap between supply and demand created by sanctions. These two points, the elasticity of demand and the availability of alternative suppliers, are closely tied together because no matter how inelastic the demand for the blockaded goods is, sanctions cannot be effective if alternate suppliers are able to provide those goods for an only marginally higher price.

The level of development of the target country is also critical. If the sanctioned country has the ability to produce the embargoed products but does not do so because it is cheaper to import them, the target will produce those goods once the sanctions succeed in raising the price of imports above the cost of domestic production. If however, the sanctioned nation does not have the technological ability to produce the embargoed products, it will be forced to turn to an alternate supplier. Therefore, we should expect economic sanctions to be most effective against underdeveloped nations that cannot supply the embargoed goods domestically under any conditions.

TESTING THE MODEL

There are essentially two types of sanctions: trade-disrupting sanctions, which affect the target country's ability to import and export, and financial sanctions aimed at reducing the target country's access to capital. Financial sanctions alone should not encourage import substitution industrialization, and for this reason may be more effective in preventing target countries from receiving economic side-benefits as the result of export sanctions. Export sanctions, however, should tend to encourage import substitution industrialization. Table 2.1 presents a set of cases which are a mix of purely financial sanctions and financial sanctions mixed with trade-disrupting sanctions. If there is a difference between financial and export sanctions in terms of the degree of import substitution industrialization they promote, it should be revealed by the mix of cases employed in this study.

The data for this study are drawn from the industrial surveys taken by the Statistical Office of the United Nations, which compiles yearly

Table 2.1
Cases

CASE	YEARS	SANCTION TYPE
U. S. vs. Dominican Rep.	1960-63	Financial, Trade
U. S. vs. Sri Lanka	1961-65	Financial
U. S. vs. Brazil	1962-64	Financial
UN vs. South Africa	1962-92	Financial, Trade
UN vs. Portugal	1963-74	Financial, Trade
U. S. vs. UAR	1963-65	Financial
U. S. vs. India	1965-67	Financial
U. K., UN vs. Rhodesia	1965-79	Financial, Trade
U. S. vs. Peru	1968-74	Financial
U. S. vs. Chile	1970-73	Financial
U. S. vs. South Korea	1973-77	Financial
U. S. vs. Turkey	1974-78	Financial
U. S. vs. Uruguay	1976-81	Financial, Trade
U. S. vs. Argentina	1977-83	Financial
Arab League vs. Egypt	1978-83	Financial, Trade
U. S. vs. Bolivia	1979-82	Financial
U. S. vs. Iran	1979-81	Financial, Trade
E.C. vs. Turkey	1980-81	Financial
U. S. vs. Poland	1980-84	Financial, Trade
U. S. vs. Syria	1980-87	Financial, Trade

Source: Hufbauer and Schott, *Economic Sanctions Reconsidered*, 1990.

and monthly data on the growth of industry and manufacturing in a selected group of countries representing various levels of development and geographic location.[6] To ensure some degree of consistency, the figures used in this study are taken from the Statistical Office's manufacturing index, which is a composite of manufacturing output, employment, and other factors indexed to a particular year for each country. The figures published by the United Nations rely on data provided by the national statistics offices, which are commissioned by the United Nations to complete the survey. It is quite likely that the data are distorted for any number of reasons; however, the use of this source is still reasonable. The various countries surveyed may have reason to distort the data they provide to the United Nations, but it is unlikely that all of the cases in this study will have distorted the data in the same manner. Therefore, unless it can be argued that sanctioned countries uniformly have an incentive to appear as though they were engaging in import substitution industrialization, it would seem unlikely that the distortions in the data will be fatal to this study.

First it must be demonstrated that the manufacturing index growth rate after sanctions exceeds the growth rate prior to trade-disrupting sanctions, and that the rate of growth increases shortly after sanctions are imposed. To compute the average growth rate before and after sanctions, two regressions were done, one for manufacturing growth for three years before sanctions and one for three years after. The slopes of each regression line were compared to determine if there was a significant effect from sanctions. The cases were then divided into different categories (see Tables 2.2 and 2.3) to test the variance in industrial growth against the type of sanction imposed on the target country, which should reveal if financial sanctions are less likely to cause import substitution industrialization than export sanctions.

Table 2. 2
Financial Sanctions

COUNTRY	OUTCOME	BEFORE	AFTER	% CHANGE
Argentina	Mixed	-1.4	-.5	64
Bolivia	Mixed	5.0	-5.8	-216
Brazil	Success	8.1	.5	-94
Chile	Success	1.6	4.2	163
India	Success	8.7	.4	-95
Peru	Success	4.7	9.2	96
S. Korea	Failure	9.7	22.9	136
Sri Lanka	Success	5.2	5.2	0
Turkey	Failure	4.0	7.4	85
Turkey 80	Success	3.1	10.1	226

Average Percent Change in Manufacturing Growth = 36%

Table 2. 3
Trade-Disrupting Sanctions

COUNTRY	OUTCOME	BEFORE	AFTER	% CHANGE
Dom. Rep.	Success	22.8	85.3	274
Egypt	Success	3.1	18.0	481
Egypt 78	Failure	5.7	10.0	75
Iran	Failure	1.6	12.3	669
Poland	Failure	.5	2.9	480
Portugal	Failure	6.9	8.6	25
Rhodesia	Mixed	7.3	13.0	78
S. Africa	Mixed	7.4	16.4	122
Syria	Failure	5.5	16.0	191
Uruguay	Mixed	3.9	6.3	62

Average Percent Change in Manufacturing Growth = 246%

It is readily apparent that many of the countries in the study experienced some type of manufacturing boom after sanctions were imposed, which is a highly counterintuitive finding in and of itself. For the cases of purely financial sanctions, the average increase in the rate of growth was 36%, but for trade and financial sanctions, the average was 246%. It is also interesting to note that the only cases in which the rate of growth in manufacturing was slower after sanctions than before were cases involving purely financial sanctions.

Trade-disrupting sanctions are worse than being merely ineffective; by encouraging import substitution they make the target country more self-sufficient and create a group of producers who have a strong financial incentive to see that sanctions remain in place. Given this, it should be no mystery why the Rump Yugoslavia was seemingly impervious to the effects of sanctions for so long. As one observer in Belgrade noted, Serbia has recently been experiencing an economic boom, which is, "probably due to the perverse effects of economic sanctions. The trade embargo has made imports some 30%-40% more expensive and encouraged the production of substitute imports."[7]

THE POLITICAL EFFECTS OF ECONOMIC SANCTIONS

So far we have explored the economic consequences of sanctions, but political effects arise from economic distortions. Trade protection, be it from sanctions or tariffs, benefits groups who own or intensively use factors of production with which, relative to the rest of the world, the country is poorly endowed. Any one of a number of exogenous factors can either cheapen or make international trade more expensive, thereby either helping or harming owners and users of relatively scarce factors.[8] Because sanctions are an exogenous factor that increase the costs of international trade, the owners and intensive users of scarce factors in that country will benefit and, consequently, will have an incentive to engage in rent-seeking behavior to ensure that their protective shield remains in place.[9]

This may help to explain why countries whose trade is distorted by economic sanctions often respond in ways that seem puzzling to outside observers, responses often labeled the "Rally around the Flag" effect and the "Fifth Column" effect.[10] The Rally effect is based on the idea that sanctions provide a common external enemy to unite the population of the target country and increase the popularity of the current leadership and its policies. While this can be seen as an irrational phenomenon, the Rally effect has, at least in some sectors, a rational economic basis. Trade-disrupting sanctions protect certain sectors of the economy that have an incentive to see that sanctions are maintained. Therefore, we should expect that those who gain from sanctions will attempt to influence the government to continue with whatever actions brought sanctions to bear against the country.[11]

Yet if sanctions create groups of gainers who benefit from sanctions, they will also harm the interests of groups that rely on imports (or export-oriented producers if the sanctions restrict the ability of the target country to export), and we should expect that these groups will organize to defend their interests. This is the economic basis of the Fifth Column effect: Sanctions will hurt key constituencies in the target country who will in turn petition their government to comply with the demands of the sender.

Unfortunately, gainers from sanctions will have two advantages over losers. First, the groups that gain from sanctions will also be gaining financial resources and should rationally be willing to expend some amount of that gain in pursuit of their interests. At the same time, groups which lose from sanctions will find themselves in a weaker financial position relative to where they stood before sanctions. Second, gainers will be a relatively small group by comparison to losers, which by the logic of collective action grants them a certain organizational advantage.[12]

There are two distinct effects commonly attributed to economic sanctions, yet are these effects contradictory and mutually exclusive, or are they complementary and simultaneous in some cases? Some have argued that the effects are possibly coexistent and that the determining factor is the severity of the sanctions imposed, but this does not appear to be supported by historical evidence.[13] Rather than simply focusing on the severity or duration of sanctions, we will begin here with the assumption that economic sanctions produce gainers and losers in the target country who can be assumed to rationally defend their interests, producing either the Rally or Fifth Column effect as a consequence (see Table 2.4).

Table 2.4
Type of Sanction and Predicted Effect

SANCTION	PREDICTED EFFECT
Financial	Fifth Column
Export	Rally
Import	Fifth Column
Financial, Export	Either
Financial, Import	Fifth Column
Export, Import	Either
Financial, Export, Import	Either

Three of these combinations produce mixed results, and the outcomes will depend on the peculiarities of the sanctions themselves and the structure of the target country's economy. Because financial sanctions will generally produce a Fifth Column effect and export sanctions will stimulate the Rally effect, when the two are combined, the outcome will be determined by the relative strength of the two types of sanctions. Strong financial sanctions combined with weak export sanctions should produce a Fifth Column effect, while weak financial sanctions and strict export sanctions should produce a Rally effect. In the other two situations, when export and import sanctions are combined, or when financial, export, and import sanctions are used together, the outcome will depend on the structure of the economy of the target country. In the case of the former, the result will depend on whether the export or import replacement sector is best able to lobby the government for favorable treatment. When all three types of sanctions are imposed simultaneously, the result will be affected by the same consideration, but with the additional element of financial sanctions, which raises transaction costs, the balance may more readily tilt in favor of the Fifth Column effect.

Several scholars have noted that domestic support for the political leadership of the target country increases in the wake of sanctions.[14] This is an understandable response; nothing brings together diverse social elements as quickly as the perception that they have been set upon by a common enemy, and sanctions can provide this common object of opprobrium. The experiences of states at war is essentially analogous. No matter what disagreement exists in the society as a whole, war against a common enemy provides a focal point to rally the population and direct their attention away from domestic issues. The Czar's decision to go to war against Germany and the Austro-Hungarian Empire in 1914 is a classic example of this sort of behavior. Realizing that the Russian Empire was close to collapsing under the weight of its internal political problems, the Czar surmised that war with Germany would unite the population and divert its attention from the ineptness of his regime. On the eve of war in July 1914, barricades were going up in the streets of the poorer sections of St. Petersburg, and it was rumored that the 1905 Soviet of Soldiers' and Workers' Deputies was about to reconvene. Yet immediately after war was declared, spontaneous nationalist demonstrations choked the streets of St. Petersburg. Representatives from all parties stumbled over each other in their rush to praise the government and declare their solidarity with a regime they had only days before been actively attacking.[15] While it ultimately led to the Czar's downfall, the war temporarily united the population for "God, Czar, and Mother Russia."

The Rally effect may operate on a similar principle, but sectors of the target country also have economically rational motivations for standing firm behind the policies that prompted the imposition of sanctions. There will be gainers and losers in any situation that alters the trade profile of a country by reducing its imports or exports. The winners in these situations where normal trade patterns have been disrupted by the distortions of economic sanctions will have an incentive to see that sanctions, and consequently the actions that brought them about, are maintained. If these winners are a significant or a well-organized group, they will be able to see to it that their interests are taken into account.[16] Import sanctions should produce a different set of winners and losers from export sanctions because they benefit domestic consumers and harm exporters. However, following the logic of collective action, it should be expected that while protected producers will rally to support the government's position, which inadvertently benefits them, consumers will not because they are a much larger group and are forced to share whatever gains result over a much larger population.[17]

This is as far as economic theory can lead us. To go further, we must turn to the historical record and see how this plays out in reality. South Africa and Rhodesia were both subject to stringent international sanctions and provide a good test of the ideas presented here. Sanctions are said to have ultimately worked in both cases; while this is true in the long run, both countries experienced distinct upswings in support for the ruling parties whose policies brought sanctions to bear. Sri Lanka, on the other hand, experienced only financial sanctions, which helped to bring to power a new government more amenable to American and British interests. While this is far too small a sample to be conclusive, these three sanctions episodes add substance to the broader set of cases.

South Africa

Various forms of sanctions were used against the Republic of South Africa since the early 1960s, but 1977 and 1986 stand out as critical years. While 1962 marks the true beginning of economic sanctions, these were often unenforced or voluntary restrictions. 1977 on the other hand, represents a significant tightening of the economic noose, imposing mandatory sanctions specifically aimed at cutting off the flow of arms and munitions to South Africa. To some extent, 1986 stands out as well: the Comprehensive Anti-Apartheid Act of 1986 imposed restrictions on U. S. trade with South Africa. In addition, as a result of growing international awareness of the inequities of the apartheid system, the mid-1980s were a period of markedly reduced investor confidence in South Africa, leading to a severe curtailment in private lending. No matter what time period we focus on, however, the purpose of sanctions throughout was to force the government of South Africa to alter its policy of apartheid and move the country in the direction of becoming a multiethnic democracy.

After 30 years of economic sanctions, South Africa renounced the racial basis of its electoral system and government, giving credence to the belief that sanctions were effective in the long run. Nelson Mandela, once a prisoner, is now president. But the question remains: Were sanctions a main catalyst of this change, or a hindrance to changes that might have taken place earlier? In the case of South Africa, the imposition and strengthening of sanctions correspond to significant shifts in support for political parties that support apartheid. While sanctions were unarguably effective in the long run, in the short and medium term they seemed to provoke a backlash against the demands of the international community, sparking a surge in support for the continuation or reinforcement of the policies that sanctions were aimed at eliminating.

The basic logic of sanctions against South Africa was that they would weaken the economy and reduce returns to capital. White South Africans control capital, and if their interests are negatively affected by sanctions, it stands to reason that they will exert political pressure on the government to change its apartheid policies to appease the international community. However, it is not at all clear that capital will be adversely affected by sanctions. We should expect that as capital becomes scarcer, returns to it will increase. So if politicians are manipulated by owners of capital, which is the link that joins sanctions-induced economic pain to political change, the effect of sanctions could be to retard the reforms that eliminate sanctions.

A tariff imposed on imports favors the intensively used factor in import-competing products. As the tariff raises import prices, it stimulates domestic production of import substitutes, and returns to the intensively used factor increase. In the case of South Africa, most of its import-competing products are capital intensive goods. Therefore, if sanctions become a trade-prohibiting tariff, they will increase returns to capital. If owners of capital behave rationally, we should expect them to pressure for the continuation or intensification of the policies that caused sanctions.

The gainers under sanctions should be those industries capable of import replacement, while the losers should be export-oriented industries. As Figure 2.2 shows, while South Africa was running a trade deficit before sanctions were tightened in 1977, imports and exports rapidly come into balance afterward.[18] What is most notable, however, is that while imports decline, exports continue to grow at approximately the same rate as before the intensification of export sanctions. This indicates that export sanctions were somewhat effective in preventing certain goods from going to South Africa, but that the import sanctions aimed at blocking South Africa's exports were not effective.

Therefore, producers of import replacement goods would have an incentive to see that sanctions are maintained so that they can continue to collect the rent imposed by sanctions, that is, the additional cost paid by South African consumers for formerly imported goods that they are now denied access to because of sanctions. While this might provoke a consumer backlash, by the logic of collective action, we can assume that the consumers will not be nearly as able to organize and petition the government for favorable policies as the smaller and better organized group of import replacement producers. In the case of the South African arms industry, which owes its very existence to sanctions, the consumer is the South African Government itself, and it was more than willing to pay the additional cost to ensure national security. On the other hand, exporters do not seem particularly disadvantaged by the sanctions and would not have an incentive to lobby for the termination of the policies that prompted sanctions.

Figure 2.2
South Africa Trade Profile

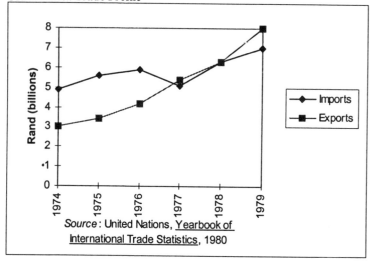

Source: United Nations, Yearbook of International Trade Statistics, 1980

Although imports declined overall, as Figure 2.3 demonstrates, imports of certain goods increased at about the time sanctions were significantly strengthened, most notably industrial parts and primary products. At the same time, imports of finished goods and capital equipment peaked immediately before the sanctions were strengthened and then declined, which could be a reflection of the import replacement pattern (see Figure 2.4). South African imports throughout the period under examination were consistently dominated by machinery, transport equipment, and other manufactured items. When sanctions were tightened, the flow of these goods decreased, but South Africa was still able to obtain primary products and parts. The fact that the importation of these items increased sharply after sanctions were imposed indicates that they were used to foster the development of import replacement industries.

Figure 2.3
Selected South African Imports

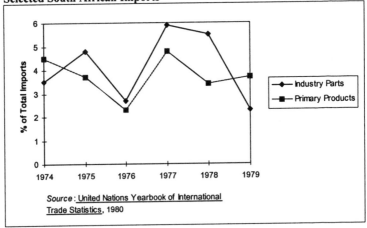

Source : United Nations Yearbook of International
Trade Statistics, 1980

Figure 2.4
South Africa Capital Equipment Imports

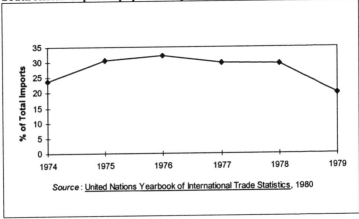

Source : United Nations Yearbook of International Trade Statistics, 1980

One of the most prominent gainers from sanctions was the South African arms industry. The Republic of South Africa had experimented with arms production before the imposition of sanctions, yet it did not receive the impetus it required to become a major industry until the United Nations Security Council imposed a total ban on arms sales to South Africa on November 4, 1977. This proved to be a fateful date in the history of South Africa, marking the beginning of a new wave of government-assisted industrialization. As a direct result of the UN sanctions, the Armaments Corporation of South Africa (ARMSCOR) was officially founded in 1977 specifically to provide for the Republic of South Africa's defense needs.

A decade later, ARMSCOR had grown from a nascent industry to one of the largest in South Africa and an important player in the highly competitive global arms market. In 1988, ARMSCOR was trading with 25 countries in small arms, artillery, and mobile artillery systems, providing the largest share of foreign exchange earnings in the manufacturing sector of the South African economy.[19] It was a major employer as well, directly and indirectly providing jobs for 90,000 individuals, making it the third or fourth largest employer in South Africa.[20]

The South African arms industry dates back to the Boer War in the 1880s, but it was only during World War II that it began to develop as an important industry. Its wartime experience convinced the South African government that in an emergency they would be unable to import the necessary components and raw materials in a timely fashion, therefore in 1948, the first of several governmental boards was established to conduct feasibility studies on the creation of an indigenous arms industry.

The first was the Defence Ordnance Workshop (now known as Lyttleton Electronics Workshop or LEW) in 1951. In the early 1960s, the Defence Ordnance Workshop expanded considerably, producing light arms under license from European manufacturers, including the Belgian FN rifle. But South Africa had yet to develop a significant arms industry. When the Belgians decided in 1964 to refuse any further orders for parts or machinery, the vulnerability of the infant industry was all too clear. By manufacturing under license, the South Africans had not developed any infrastructure or trained design personnel.

At about the same time, international pressure against South Africa began to intensify. In 1962, the United Nations Security Council received the first of many appeals to ban the sale of military equipment to South Africa, but the supply of arms was not dramatically affected. However, these incidents foreshadowed what was to come and only made the South African leadership more aware of their vulnerability, and increased their resolve to attain self-sufficiency in strategic industries. The political trends in Africa only intensified this resolve. The early 1960s saw a virtual explosion of new states in the African continent as the process of decolonization gained momentum, and many of these new states were of a distinctly leftist character, which the South African government saw as a potential threat. In the context of the Cold War, the South African government perceived itself to be, along with Rhodesia and the remaining Portuguese colonies, the only reliable balance against a communist-dominated Africa. Therefore, South African national security extended well beyond merely securing the borders and providing for internal security against African liberation movements, such as the African National Congress.

1964 was a watershed year for the South African arms industry. Not only did Belgium break its ties, but both Britain and the United States implemented restrictions of varying severity. Britain suspended nearly 100 arms manufacturing licenses and the United States cut off arms manufacturing assistance. These actions prompted the South African Parliament to pass the Armaments Act in 1964, which shifted the balance of arms procurement and production from the public to the private sector. The Armaments Act created a Munitions Production Board with heavy private sector representation, thus establishing a strong link between South African national security and the interests of the private manufacturing sector.

Over the next decade, international revulsion with the system of apartheid grew, finally culminating with the Sharpeville massacre and the death of Steven Biko in 1976 and 1977 respectively. In response to these actions, the UN Security Council imposed a total arms embargo on South Africa on November 4, 1977. The embargo was mandatory for all members of the UN and was designed to cut off the supply of all strategic materials to South Africa in the hopes that this would force the South African government to moderate its racial policies.

The South African government, however, saw the arms embargo in a completely different light. Given the regional situation, and the high level of Soviet and Soviet client state activity in the region, South Africa was not about to allow any international protests affect its ability to guard against these threats. The Soviet Union was directly involved in Ethiopia, while Cuba had committed upwards of 40,000 combat troops to the Angolan civil war. In addition, there were other Soviet clients involved in these conflicts, especially East Germany and Czechoslovakia. South Africa saw itself with no choice but to intensively develop an arms industry to defend against these threats. South Africa already had a developed industrial base and established industries in steel, heavy equipment, and explosives. A means of coordinating and organizing these industries was needed to create a self-sufficient arms industry capable of supplying the South African Defence Forces.[21]

The was partially accomplished through the creation of the Munitions Production Board in 1964, and in 1968, the Armaments Development and Production Corporation of South Africa, which later became ARMSCOR. Under this new framework, Lyttelton Engineering Works and Pretoria Metal Pressings were privatized and became subsidiaries of this government/private industry collaboration. A year later, Armaments Development developed its own aircraft division, Atlas Aircraft Corporation, and became a major shareholder in Ronden, an explosives manufacturer. In rapid succession, Armaments Development acquired hunting rifle manufacturers and two chemical factories important in the production of propellants and high explosives. In 1970, Armaments Development was able to produce over 100 types of ammunition, but still relied on external sources for aircraft, ships and armored vehicles.[22] Once a complete ban on military items was imposed in 1977, Armaments Development became ARMSCOR, and began to reach into new territory such as ships, aircraft, armored vehicles, and support items. As a result of sanctions, South Africa went from being a buyer on the arms market, dependent on foreign-produced goods for its national security, to being not only self-sufficient, but also a major exporter of highly advanced conventional weapons such as the G-7 self-contained mobile artillery unit.

If trade distortions in the form of sanctions produce gainers such as ARMSCOR, then they should also produce losers who will pressure the government to abandon the policies that prompted sanctions. The losers in this case were expected to be South Africa's exporters, who were ostensibly harmed by the refusal of other nations to buy their products. South Africa's main exports are primarily extractive, specifically gold, diamonds, and other rare items such as uranium and titanium. The three largest exports in terms of dollar value from South Africa are nonferrous metals, coal, and iron.[23] But South Africa's gross volume of exports increased throughout the sanctions period, indicating that on an aggregate level sanctions had no net negative effect on South African exports. If this is true, then exporters should not have had any reason to pressure the government for changes in the apartheid system, which was the cause of sanctions. At the same time, import replacement industries had every reason to take steps to see that sanctions were maintained. It remains to be seen, however, if this had any effect on South Africa's political response to sanctions.

There were three major parties or coalitions in South Africa.[24] The National Party (NP) was the ruling party since 1948 and is the architect of apartheid, the policy that sanctions were aimed at eliminating.

Figure 2.5
South Africa Elections

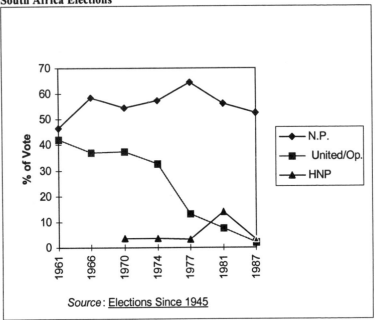

Source: Elections Since 1945

United/Opposition is the coalition that contested most of the post-war elections. While it is an amalgamation of parties, some of which supported and some of which opposed apartheid, United/Opposition stands as the only party that at some time opposed apartheid. HNP (Herstigte Nasional Partei) ran on the platform of not only maintaining the current policies of apartheid but actually intensifying them by introducing additional restrictions on the Black South African population. As we can see in Figure 2.5 support for the National Party increased after sanctions were imposed in 1962. At the same time, support for the United/Opposition block declined after both 1962 and 1977. Perhaps the most striking aspect of this trend toward more conservative parties is the rise of HNP. While its support was minuscule in the early part of the 1970s, it increases dramatically after 1977. Most of its support was drawn away from the National Party, which began, at least in the eyes of the HNP, to show signs of weakening apartheid restrictions.

Eventually, of course, South Africa eliminated apartheid commenced the process of becoming a multiethnic democracy. Sanctions had some influence on the outcome in the long run but in the short term, they seem to have been counterproductive. When sanctions were imposed and later strengthened, support for parties in favor of the policies that prompted sanctions increased, while support for the parties that opposed those policies declined. At the same time, a party whose platform revolved around the idea of intensifying apartheid scored major gains. While ultimately the National Party and the South African government abandoned apartheid, there was a rally effect that correlated strongly with the dates when sanctions were imposed or strengthened. Still, one might contend that the Rally effect had nothing to do with the fact that sanctions appeared to benefit import replacement producers without harming exporters. Although it cannot be proven that there was a direct link between the two, it is obvious given the shift in South Africa's trade profile that certain industries benefited from sanctions and would therefore have an incentive to see that sanctions were maintained.

Rhodesia (Zimbabwe)

The case of Rhodesia presents another instance in which both financial and trade-disrupting sanctions were used. Rhodesia, like South Africa, featured a white minority that controlled virtually every political office in the country. After experiencing pressure from the United Kingdom to broaden its political system to include the non-European majority, the Rhodesian government led by Ian Smith unilaterally declared its independence from the United Kingdom (UK) in 1965. In response, the UK, later assisted by the United Nations, imposed sanctions designed to deny Rhodesia access to imported goods, cut off the traditional markets for Rhodesian exports, and prevented Rhodesia from receiving financial assistance and credits on the international market. Her Majesty's government was confident that these measures would bring its recalcitrant former colony into line.

Despite the best efforts of the international community to wreak havoc on the Rhodesian economy and force the white minority to vote the Smith government from power, support for the Smith government and his Rhodesian Front party actually increased throughout the 1960s.[25] While this was exactly the opposite response of what was expected, it fits the model rather well. Rhodesian industry boomed in the face of sanctions, which may provide a rational explanation for the enduring popularity of the Smith government.

Although export industries lost, their losses were mitigated by the fact that much of the employment and capital that went into producing exports before sanctions were transferred to import replacement industries. As one contemporary observer noted, "The imposition of rigid import controls, especially on consumer goods, necessitated by the fall in exports, has led to considerable import substitution. New firms have begun and old ones expanded to provide employment for whites. White employment increased in every quarter from 1965 to 1968."[26] In addition to absorbing existing white unemployment resulting from sanctions, import replacement industries were also providing jobs for the 6,000 white immigrants who came to Rhodesia during the first two years of sanctions. The end result was that, "On urban white workers, therefore, the effects of sanctions were very much reduced. It is this group on which Mr. Smith has come to rely for the bulk of his political support."[27]

The Rhodesian government was able to simultaneously shift the burden of sanctions onto the black population and reap political rewards in the form of increased support from the white population. "Not only did the responsibility for economic damage in Rhodesia clearly lie with Britain's imposing sanctions, but also the Rhodesian government was able to shift most of the burden to sections of the population whose discontent would not endanger the regime."[28] Rhodesia's main exports prior to sanctions were tobacco and minerals, both of which used large amounts of black labor. As these export-oriented extractive industries were weakened by sanctions, capital and white labor shifted to import replacement industries, but for the most part, black labor did not. In this manner the Smith government was able to keep its white urban base of support, while shifting the bulk of the burden to the rural black population.

Sanctions forced the development of new industries and reduced Rhodesia's traditional dependence on the export of a few basic commodities. In 1966, observers of the Rhodesian economy noted that "local industry has not been severely damaged. Reports of expansion plans by several firms indicate the degree of confidence in parts of the private sector... on the whole it has been reported that 80 new factories have been established during the first quarter of this year."[29] An earlier report found that while traditional exports such as tobacco and minerals exports fell dramatically under sanctions, there was evidence of a "long-term gain to Rhodesia by switching over from an exporter in essential metals to a processor for local secondary industries (which) would prove invaluable for domestic development."[30] While financial sanctions against Rhodesia should have been effective, they were subverted by South Africa, which operated as a financial waystation for funds ultimately destined for Rhodesia. But these sanctions could merely be said to be ineffective because sufficient international cooperation was not achieved. It was the trade-distorting sanctions that proved to be a boost to the development of the Rhodesian economy, forcing it to diversify and produce a wider range of secondary products.

Another interesting trend to note in the Rhodesian case is that the white urban base of support for the Smith government actual grew during the sanctions period because of increased white immigration. This fact presents an interesting paradox: why would anyone want to move to a country experiencing some of the most stringent economic sanctions ever imposed? Given the prominence afforded the conflict between the international community and the Smith government, it would not be an unfair assumption that white immigrants to Rhodesia during the sanctions period were supporters of the Smith government while emigrants were more likely to be opponents. Yet despite sanctions, immigration outweighed emigration between 1965 and 1975, with the exception of 1966 (see Figure 2.6). If immigrants supported the Smith regime, and emigrants tended to be its detractors, then the Smith regime would have experienced a surge in support for its policies during the sanctions period. This was clearly the opposite of what sanctions were supposed to do, yet the evidence presented here suggests that this is what occurred.

Figure 2.6

Rhodesian Migration 1962-1977

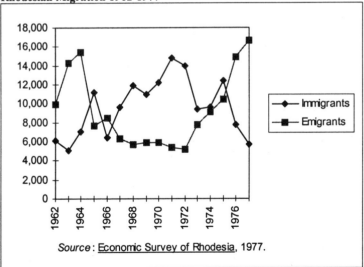

Source: Economic Survey of Rhodesia, 1977.

Figure 2.7
Rhodesian Front Membership 1962-1968

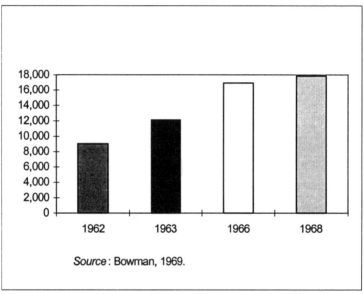

Source: Bowman, 1969.

Most importantly, as shown in Figure 2.7, support for the Rhodesian Front, the party responsible for the actions that brought sanctions to bear against Rhodesia, increased immediately after sanctions were imposed. The Rhodesian Front authored the Unilateral Declaration of Independence (UDI), which was the initial cause of sanctions, and was adamantly against any sort of compromise solution that would allow greater nonwhite participation in the political system. Yet it grew steadily more popular through the 1960s and experienced its greatest increase in membership immediately after sanctions were imposed in 1965. This Rally effect is consistent with what the model would predict and helps to explain the puzzled contemporary accounts. After sanctions had been in place for nearly a year, it was noted that, "There is no sign that the international sanctions campaign--which is undeniably 'biting' on the Rhodesian economy--is having a political impact. The growing economic distress it is causing is not being accompanied by a political reaction against Mr. Smith. The white population continued to show overwhelming support for Mr. Smith."[31]   Although sanctions were undoubtedly "biting," the bite was offset by gains from import substitution industrialization. Although in this case it is not clear if import replacement industries gained more than export industries lost, it is evident that there was a transfer of labor and capital from the export sector to the import replacement sector that at least partially offset the losses to the export sector, making whatever burden Rhodesia had to endure more palatable.

As in the case of South Africa, Rhodesia eventually relented and held multiracial elections. It is highly questionable if sanctions had much effect on this outcome. The protracted civil war and the loss of colonial allies in former Portuguese territory of Mozambique did much more to weaken the Smith government than sanctions. Even if sanctions did contribute to the end result, the fact remains that for years the Rhodesian economy blossomed, and political support for Ian Smith and his policies increased.

These cases indicate that export sanctions can produce a Rally effect that runs counter to the sender's expectations and desires. In both cases, the senders imposed sanctions with the expectations that economic deprivation would force the respective governments to alter their political systems to enfranchise and incorporate the non-European majority. Both of these attempts to use economic pressure provoked a backlash that is reflected in the electoral and party membership records of parties that supported the policies that sanctions were aimed at eliminating. Although this Rally effect may be simply an expression of nationalism in response to foreign pressure, there is some evidence that it is linked to the distortions in trade induced by sanctions. By creating an opportunity for import replacement industries to fill the gap between supply and demand, sanctions create a constituency that has a vested interest in seeing that sanctions and the policies that prompted them remain in place.

Sri Lanka

In January 1961, the Socialist government of Sirvamo Bandaranaike created the Ceylon Petroleum Corporation and then proceeded to expropriate the assets of American and British oil companies operating in Ceylon (Sri Lanka) valued at approximately $12 million. In 1962, the Ceylon Petroleum Corporation expropriated privately owned service stations and concluded oil deals with the Soviet Union and Romania. In the same year, the Hickenlooper amendment, which bars aid to countries that expropriate American property was signed into law. After a series of fruitless negotiations over compensation, the United States suspended all economic aid in February 1963.

Sri Lanka was subjected to financial sanctions which, according to the model, should not produce any gainers from sanctions. Unlike export sanctions, financial sanctions do not produce a group of import replacement producers who stand to gain from the maintenance of sanctions. What financial sanctions should do, however, is weaken investor confidence and generally harm the business environment. They harm most producer groups and should not benefit any group in particular; therefore, in this case we should see a Fifth Column effect, or at the very least, the absence of a Rally effect.

The termination of U. S. aid had a heavy negative impact on the Sri Lankan economy as the reduction in anticipated income forced the government to find revenue from other sources. New taxes were imposed in 1963 to partially cover the burgeoning budget deficit, which had "risen again as a result of the suspension of American aid."[32] These new taxes took their toll politically and evoked "strong opposition to the government's increased deficit financing."[33] In addition to the new wave of taxation, the Sri Lankan government imposed import controls in an effort to stem the flow of hard currency leaving the country and began to engage in barter exchanges of raw materials for imports, both of which had a tendency to force up the cost of living.[34] Although wages increased, they could not keep up with the cost of living increases, resulting in severe inflation. In 1963, Sri Lanka experienced an economic disaster: The cost of living was at its highest level ever while the money supply and unemployment continued to spiral upward.[35] These events led to the gloomy assessment in late 1964 that "The economy is suffering from a general malaise bred by the private sector's lack of confidence in the future."[36] Sanctions clearly had a major negative impact on the Sri Lankan economy and this was reflected in the fortunes of the ruling political party in the 1965 elections.

Figure 2.8
Sri Lanka Elections 1952-1965

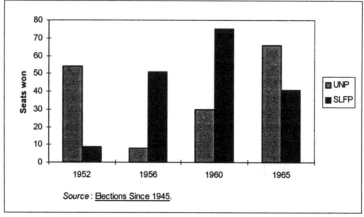

Source: Elections Since 1945.

The United National Party (UNP) was one of Sri Lanka's two main political parties, a historically conservative party with an urban elite support base. The Sri Lanka Freedom Party (SLFP) was the UNP's main opposition, espousing a more leftist doctrine and finding its base of support in the countryside. For our purposes, however, the critical issue is where the two parties stood on the issue that prompted the imposition of sanctions and, in turn, how they faired in the election of 1965 (see Figure 2.8). The United States imposed sanctions in response to the Sri Lankan government's expropriation without compensation of several oil refinery facilities owned by U. S. and British companies. When the expropriations occurred in 1961, the SLFP was in power, but at the next parliamentary election, it suffered a major defeat, which was at least partially due to sanctions.

The financial sanctions aimed at Sri Lanka revolved around U. S. aid money and World Bank loans that were denied or delayed as a result of Sri Lanka's expropriations. U. S. aid declined from $17.7 million in 1959 to $3.9 million in 1965, and the World Bank declared Sri Lanka "no longer creditworthy" after announcing that the bank would no longer lend to countries that expropriate without compensation.[37] As one observer notes, "The coerciveness of the sanctions against Ceylon lay in the intensification of the economic decline and, most critically, in the withholding of that help which the Ceylonese saw as the only way of arresting the deterioration of their economy."[38] Sanctions had a negative effect on the already troubled Sri Lankan economy as the cutback in the flow of foreign assistance drained its international reserves, which fell from $236 million in 1956 to $73 million in 1965.[39]. This fomented an economic crisis and, as a result, Sri Lanka ultimately complied with the United States' demands for compensation.

The most critical point for the purposes of this investigation is the fact that sanctions played a role in the downfall of the SLFP in the 1965 election. Because of the economic crisis, the UNP was able to make sanctions a major issue in the elections and, as a consequence, one of its campaign promises was to resolve the expropriation issue "within 24 hours." [40] The UNP more or less kept its promise and reached an agreement to pay compensation shortly after it won the election. As a result, aid quickly returned to pre-sanctions levels. Once again, the case seems to fit the predictions of the model well. Financial sanctions imposed a cost without benefiting any particular sector, therefore there was no incentive for any group to lobby for the maintenance of the policies that prompted sanctions. The case could be made that the SLFP with its generally socialist program may have driven the Sri Lankan economy into the ground without the help of sanctions. While this may be true, it is still the fact that aid, which the government was counting on to maintain some stability in the economy, was not forthcoming, and this had a discernible effect that directly led to the downfall of the SLFP.

Sanctions are imposed with almost no regard for the effects they might actually have and the danger that they may do more harm than good. It is simply inaccurate to state that sanctions are always useless, but by the same token, we can no longer afford to ignore the fact that sanctions can have serious counterproductive effects. In order to resolve the issue of effectiveness, it is first necessary to disaggregate sanctions and look at how different types of sanctions effect the economy of the target country. Politics and economics are fundamentally linked, and whenever trade or capital flows are interrupted to any significant degree, there will be some sort of political response. The critical question is whether that response will be one that conforms to the desires of the sender or one that directly counters them. By disaggregating sanctions and predicting the effects that different sanctions should have, this chapter offers some basis for the use of financial sanctions over the use of trade-disrupting sanctions.

NOTES

1. Because every case involving import sanctions also featured export sanctions, I grouped the two together as trade-disrupting sanctions. While this does not allow us to separate out the effects of import and export sanctions, we can still distinguish between the purely financial and trade-disrupting varieties. The fact that import and export sanctions cannot be separated does not reduce the validity of the argument, because if there is any difference in the amount of import substitution, it can only be the result of export sanctions. Denying a country access to the global marketplace (import sanctions) would not spur an increase in industrial production.

2. Geoffrey Brunn, *Europe and the French Imperium* (New York: Harper and Row, 1938), 97.

3. Ibid., 99.

4. Richard Overy, *The Road to War* (London: BBC Books, 1989), 41.

5. Burton Klein, *Germany's Economic Preparations for War* (Cambridge, Harvard University Press, 1959), 207.

6. Statistical Office of the United Nations, *Yearbook of Industrial Statistics: Growth in World Industry* (New York: United Nations 1965-1985).

7. "Serbia's Economy" *The Economist,* 7 May 1994, p. 60.

8. Ronald Rogowski, *Commerce and Coalitions: How Trade Affects Domestic Political Alignments* (Princeton: Princeton University Press, 1989).

9. Arnold Harberger, "Monopoly and Resource Allocation," *American Economic Review* 44, no. 2 (1954): 77-87; Anne Krueger, "The Political Economy of the Rent Seeking Society," *American Economic Review* 64, no. 3

(1974): 291-303; Jonathan Pincus, "Pressure Groups and the Pattern of Tariffs," *Journal of Political Economy,* 83, no. 4 (1975): 757-778; Robert Tollinson, "Rent Seeking: A Survey," *Kyklos* 35, no. 4 (1982): 575-602.

10. United States General Accounting Office, *Economic Sanctions: Effectiveness as Tools of Foreign Policy.* Report to the Chairman, Committee on Foreign Relations, U. S. Senate. Washington D.C. (February 1992) GAO/NSIAD-92-106.

11. The implicit assumption here is that the state is a support-maximizing entity. See R. Peltzman, "Towards a More General Theory of Regulation," *Journal of Law and Economics* 19, no. 1 (1976).

12. Mancur Olson, *The Logic of Collective Action:Public Goods and the Theory of Groups* (Cambridge: Harvard University Press, 1971).

13. United States General Accounting Office, Report to the Chairman, Committee on Foreign Relations, U. S. Senate, *Economic Sanctions: Effectiveness as Tools of Foreign Policy,* February 1992.

14. T. Willett and M. Jalaighajar, "U. S. Trade Policy and National Security," *Cato Journal* 3, no. 3 (1983): 717-28.

15. Ward Rutherford, *The Russian Army in World War I* (London: Cremonisi Publishers, 1975), 5.

16. David Rowe has developed this argument to its fullest extent to date. According to his model, export sanctions introduce a distortion in the market for imports that benefit certain strong constituencies and induce political behavior that may be counter to the interests of the sender. See, *The Domestic Political Economy of International Economic Sanctions,* Center for International Affairs Working Paper, No. 93-1, Harvard University, 1993.

17. The same reason that tariffs, which restrict free trade to the detriment of consumers can exist can be used to illustrate this point. If the United States imposes a tariff on sugar of five cents per pound, the increase in price at the supermarket would hardly be noticeable. At the same time, the benefits to domestic sugar producers would be huge. While we can expect that sugar producers will lobby for the continuation of the tariff, it is hardly worth the effort of individual consumers to lobby against it.

18. Data for this section and other case studies in this chapter are drawn from *Yearbook of International Trade Statistics,* Statistical Office of the United Nations, New York, various issues 1960-1984.

19. "Company of the Year: ARMSCOR," *Engineering Week* (March, 1989): 2.

20. James P. McWilliams, *ARMSCOR: South Africa's Arms Merchant* (London: Brassey's Press, 1989), 7.

21. "Country Survey: South Africa," *Jane's Defence Weekly,* 20 July 1991, p. 2-3.

22. "Company of the Year," p. 2.

23. United States General Accounting Office, Report to Congressional Requesters: *South Africa, Trends in Trade, Lending and Investment,* (Washington, D.C: April 1988), 11.

24. Ian Gorvin, ed., *Elections Since 1945* (Chicago: St. James Press, 1989), 311.

25. Larry W. Bowman, "Organization, Power and Decision-Making Within the Rhodesian Front," *Journal of Commonwealth Studies* 7, no. 2 (1969): 145-65.

26. R. B. Sutcliffe, "The Political Economy of Economic Sanctions," p.119.

27. Ibid.

28. Ibid., 114.

29. Economist Intelligence Unit, *Quarterly Economic Review of Rhodesia, Zambia and Malawi,* 54 (May 1966): 7.

30. Economist Intelligence Unit, *Quarterly Economic Review of Rhodesia, Zambia and Malawi,* 53 (February 1966): 8.

31. Economist Intelligence Unit, *Quarterly Economic Review of Rhodesia, Zambia and Malawi,* 55 (August 1966): 2.

32. Economist Intelligence Unit, *Quarterly Economic Review of Ceylon,* 41 (March, 1963): 4.

33. Economist Intelligence Unit, *Quarterly Economic Review of Ceylon,* 42 (May, 1963): 2.

34. Economist Intelligence Unit, *Quarterly Economic Review of Ceylon,* 41 (March, 1963): 5.

35. Economist Intelligence Unit, *Quarterly Economic Review of Ceylon,* 45 (March , 1964): 4.

36. Economist Intelligence Unit, *Quarterly Economic Review of Ceylon,* 48 (November, 1964): 4.

37. Richard Olson, "Expropriation and International Economic Coercion: Ceylon and the West 1961-65," *Journal of Developing Areas* 11, no. 2 (1977): 211-212.

38. Ibid., 225.

39. Ibid., 214.

40. Ibid., 217.

3

The American Embargo of Great Britain, 1807-1811

States have consistently used economic means to influence other actors in the international system since the Peloponnesian Wars. What has changed over time is how sanctions are used. For centuries, mercantilist principles dictated that trade benefited the seller and exploited the buyer. Napoleon's continental system, for example, denied the British access to continental markets while allowing continental exports to Britain.[1] In the modern era, however, sanctions are generally used to block exports to a targeted country. The historical record does not contain many examples of sanctions being used in this manner, but the American embargo of Great Britain from 1807 to 1811 closely parallels the way in which economic sanctions are used today. Its effects are therefore not only of historical importance, but they also offer compelling evidence for how and why economic sanctions do and do not work in the current international system.

Because of the nature of trade between the United States and Great Britain at the time, British agriculture was the prime beneficiary from American sanctions. Britain imported mainly cotton and grains from the United States, so a severe disruption in the flow of trade would boost the price of grain. British landed interests would then have an incentive to see that the cause of American indignation was not removed and to take action in Parliament to see that their interests were upheld.

In fact, this is precisely what occurred. The issue in question was the Orders in Council (OIC) of 1807, which mandated the British navy to seize cargoes of neutral ships bound for continental Europe. This was clearly a violation of neutral shipping rights and, as the United States was the major neutral carrier at the time, the impact of the OIC fell heavily on the American maritime economy. American sanctions, therefore, were intended to force the repeal of the OIC. The issue of whether to do so was the topic of debates in both the House of Commons and the House of Lords, and as is clearly revealed in the following analysis, Members of Parliament representing agricultural regions that benefited from the reduced trade with the United States were much more supportive of maintaining or intensifying the OIC, while their counterparts from more industrial areas were by and large in favor of repealing them.

This analysis essentially involves the use of a modern public choice model in the study of early nineteenth century Great Britain, which could legitimately be questioned. Public choice models are generally used to explain events in societies with well-developed pressure groups, and Great Britain, especially before the Reform Act of 1832, could hardly be considered a modern democracy by any measure. This does not mean, however, that pressure groups did not arise to defend their interests or that members of Parliament did not represent the interests of their constituencies, however limited they might be in comparison to the general population. In a study of the causes of British trade liberalization in the 1840s, Cheryl Schoenhardt Bailey found that a public choice model was applicable to the actions of the Anti-Corn Law League and that the economic composition of the parliamentary district was a good predictor of how the member of Parliament from that district voted on trade liberalization issues.[2] Therefore, even if public choice models developed to explain U. S. trade policy in the late twentieth century do not mesh perfectly with the political realities of nineteenth-century Britain, there is evidence that they function reasonably well as a tool to aid in the explanation of events from that period.

The purpose here is not to explain the repeal of the Corn Laws but rather to explain why the British government in the early 1800s refused to relax its hostile stance toward neutral shipping in the face of sanctions from the country most harmed by this action, the United States. The United States imposed an embargo on all economic exchange with Britain in 1807 in the hope that it would harm British exporters' interests to the point that they would pressure Parliament for the repeal of the OIC. Instead, the British government did nothing of the kind, leaving the orders in place and waiting until the American government gave up on the embargo in the face of domestic pressure that made its maintenance politically impossible.

There are several explanations as to why this occurred, yet none are completely satisfactory. First, most of the historical research on the events of that time suggests that the embargo hurt the United States more than Britain and was detrimental to the interests of influential groups in the United States, namely the entire New England maritime economy. This interpretation has been brought into question by historians who have calculated the actual economic damage to Britain and determined it to be quite significant. "The Embargo was in fact an effective weapon," argues Jeffrey Frankel. "It failed through a lack of political will and perseverance to use it rather than through a lack of economic power."[3] A true embargo would bring both countries to a state of autarchy with regard to each other, which is more or less what occurred. The real value of American goods entering Britain in the year ending 5 January 1809 fell from £6,531,410 the year before to £1,751,986, a decline of 73%. Exports from Britain to the United States fell from £12,097,942 to £5,302,866, a decline of 58%. This severe reduction in trade had serious effects on a trade-based economy such as Britain's, especially since it were unable to trade openly with continental Europe at this time. In addition, this explanation focuses on the American side of the relationship, and while it may explain why the United States dropped the embargo, it does not explain why Britain, in the absence of any knowledge that the United States would blink first, refused to remove the Orders in Council despite the fact it was harming Britain's export interests.

Figure 3.1
Wheat Prices in Britain 1804-1811

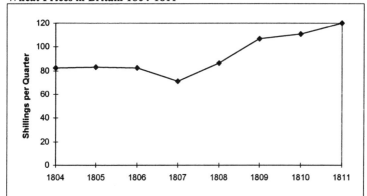

Source: Abstract of British Historical Statistics, 1962

As Figure 3.1 demonstrates, wheat prices rose significantly following the imposition of the American embargo. British wheat producers were able to sell their grain for nearly 50 percent more in 1809 than in 1807, an increase that is directly attributable to the sanctions. Clearly the continuance of the policies that kept the American embargo in place was in the best interests of British wheat producers. On the other side of the equation, British manufacturing interests, which were harmed by the American embargo, should have pressured their representatives to seek the termination of the Orders in Council responsible for the loss of the American market.

The British-American relationship, however, must be set within the greater context of the Napoleonic Wars. At the same time the United States engaged Britain in economic warfare, France was attempting to strangle British commerce in a somewhat different manner. While America used both import and export sanctions, the French relied primarily on import sanctions. France was quite willing to sell French goods to England, (provided the goods met with Napoleon's licensing requirements) but tried to starve the commercial base of the British economy by blocking the entrance of British goods into continental Europe. Although this seems at odds with the modern definition of a blockade, economic warfare strategists of the time operated under mercantilist assumptions. The concept of mutually beneficial trade was not yet generally accepted, and trade was seen as an act that benefited the seller, not the buyer. Therefore, Napoleon's sanctions and the British retaliation were aimed at blocking each other's ability to export, thus denying the enemy the profits from trade.

British vessels were allowed by their own government to trade with the continent, the only exception being the sale of military goods. Even this prohibition, however, was somewhat flexible. It was noted in Parliament in 1812 that "the clothing of the French Army came from Yorkshire and not only the accouterment, but the ornaments of Marshall Soult and his army came from Birmingham."[4] In a similar manner, French authorities allowed a fair amount of continental goods to flow to Britain, provided the outgoing ships brought back gold or commercial paper home in return.[5] Clearly, the focus of economic warfare during the Napoleonic Wars was what would today be referred to as import sanctions.

Napoleon's Berlin Decree of 1806, which declared Britain to be in a state of blockade, was the beginning of a new round of economic warfare between the two countries. The Berlin Decree supposedly prohibited all trade with the enemy, but the reality of the situation was that Napoleon simply lacked the naval power after Trafalgar to enforce a blockade at sea. The blockade had to be applied on land and was "aimed at being a self-blockade on the part of the continent."[6] The reasoning was that Britain would soon find itself in dire economic circumstances if it could not sell to the continent. To some extent Napoleon was correct, but British commerce continued to flow to the continent via smugglers and neutral carriers, and British merchants opened new markets in the Americas, which absorbed some of the goods that would have gone to the continent under normal circumstances.

The British reaction to the Berlin Decree was to use any way possible to compel the French to revoke their self-imposed blockade. The British did not respond in kind immediately but did try to injure French and allied states' trade. With British mastery of the high seas a given after the 1805 devastation of the French fleet at Trafalgar, French trading ships did not dare to venture beyond the coastal waters. This placed the neutral states in a critical role. The United States was the principal neutral state at the time, and its merchant fleet grew tremendously as a result of the economic warfare between Britain and France.

Subsequent attempts by the British to suppress the neutral shipping that frustrated their attempts to reduce continental exports ultimately led to the Orders in Council which provoked American sanctions. In 1807, Napoleon issued two decrees from Milan. The first strengthened the economic actions against Britain; the second was a direct response to a British Order in Council that specified all neutral ships bound for the continent must stop in Britain first. This drove Napoleon to declare in the second Milan Decree that any ship that did so would be considered British and thus subject to confiscation. The American merchant marine was placed in a quandary. If it obeyed British restrictions, American ships and cargoes would be seized by French authorities on arrival; however, if they observed French regulations, there was a strong chance that the ship and its cargo would be seized by the British navy.

To remove itself from this unviable situation, the American government decided to impose sanctions against Britain rather than France. There are several possible reasons for this demonstration of favoritism toward France. The most basic is that only a few decades earlier, France had helped the United States gain its freedom from Britain and the current president, Jefferson, was favorably disposed toward France in general. The other possibility is that the French policy was not nearly so noxious. It merely demanded that on any particular voyage, neutrals have no intercourse with Britain prior to landing in a French-controlled port. British policy, on the other hand, destroyed the profitable continental trade for the United States. The choice seemed easy for America: If it could force a change in British policy, it could still enjoy profitable relations with Europe. Forcing Napoleon to revoke the Milan

Decree would not have the same effect as long as Britain maintained its policy.

Despite the obvious importance of Napoleon's actions and the continental system, this chapter focuses on the American sanctions against Britain for two reasons. First, American sanctions, unlike Napoleon's, were not aimed at weakening Britain in general, but rather were imposed with the intention of forcing Britain to retract the OIC, which were the source of American irritation. The nature of American sanctions, therefore, provide us with a discreet means for measuring the effects of sanctions as opposed to the general goals of the Continental System. Second, American sanctions were both import and export, while Napoleon relied mainly on import sanctions. Therefore, by focusing on the American-British relationship, we can most effectively judge the effects of different types of sanctions.

BRITISH RELATIONS WITH THE UNITED STATES AND THE ORDERS IN COUNCIL

The American Revolution raised a number of questions as to how trade was to be conducted between Great Britain and her former colony. Some in Parliament wanted to treat the United States as any other country, but others wanted to offer concessions to prevent France or Holland from making incursions into what had been a lucrative market for British manufacturers and merchants.[7] The British negotiator James Fox was of a liberal bent but was set upon by interest groups "determined to resist the terms of the preliminary articles of peace."[8] Fox persuaded Parliament to grant the government the power to regulate trade with the United States by Orders in Council, which were constructed to allow American ships to land in British and West Indian ports on terms that the British considered generous even if their former colony did not. The United States demanded full reciprocity, which the powerful British shipping interests in competition with American shipping would not allow, so the OIC became the means of regulating trade with America without parliamentary battles for decades to come.

Interest group lobbying efforts were prominently displayed over this issue. The United States was particularly dissatisfied with an OIC in December 1783 that forbade it to trade directly with the West Indies, but it was British shipping interests led in part by Lord Sheffield who led the drive for these restrictions. Sheffield and his allies insisted that because the U. S. had rejected colonial status and because the monopoly of trade was the prime justification for the expense of maintaining colonies, Britain should protect its monopoly of the West Indian trade from American commercial incursions.[9] The shipping interests tried to convince the manufacturers that they would profit from the OIC because the use of British ships would "give an opportunity to British merchants to vend a much greater quantity of our manufactures in purchasing American produce for the West India market."[10]

This meant that the Americans were forced to look elsewhere since they could not trade as readily with the British Caribbean colonies as they would have liked. America began trading with the East Indies, but that was severely constrained by the East India Company, which restricted American shipping to direct voyages to and from the United States. Given the difficulty of engaging in trade, the United States encouraged domestic manufacturing to fill in the gap and reduce the outflow of specie. Obviously, the harmonious and mutually beneficial trade that Fox and other liberals had hoped for was not to be. Tensions between the United States and Britain only increased as a long-promised commercial treaty was continually put on hold and compensation debt issues stemming from the American Revolution were brought to the fore. The American government (or more realistically, governments, as the confederation of the early post-revolution period placed the balance of power in each individual state capital) responded with additional duties on British shipping and other means of retaliation for the British Navigation Acts.[11] British merchants were understandably upset over this treatment but there was little the federal government could do until the new constitution was adopted in 1789. Even then, however, tensions still ran high and were brought to a boiling point by the British denial of neutral shipping rights during the war with France. A crisis was temporarily avoided when the British conceded on a number of points, including the right of American ships to trade in the East Indies and an extension of American rights in the West Indies, but these measures did not completely mollify the Americans. Even so, trade between the two countries expanded to the point that in 1800 British exports to the United States were double that of only seven years before.[12]

As these events indicate, the conflict between the United States and Britain over neutral shipping rights during the Napoleonic wars was not without precedent. There was a long history of hostility between the two nations arising from the schizoid desire of the United States to be treated both as a sovereign country and retain preferential trading rights with Britain, as well as Britain's condescending treatment of its former colony. When war broke out between France and Britain in 1793, economic warfare became a central component of the belligerents' attempts to strangle each other, which inevitably affected the United States, the leading neutral carrier.[13] Once again British shipping interests, this time led by James Stephen, took the lead in protecting their interests under the guise of national security. In concert with West Indian interests, Stephen argued that only a complete prohibition of neutral carriers from transshipping French and Spanish colonial products through the United States to Britain would protect the nation.[14] British manufacturers were concerned that the interference with neutral shipping rights would provoke an American reaction against British imports so "the issue was clearly joined... between the interests of commerce depending upon exports and shipping, upon which it was alleged that the safety of the nation depended."[15]

This pattern was to be repeated. British shipping interests pressed for more stringent restrictions on neutral shipping rights using the fig leaf of national security to cover their blatant interests in protecting their monopoly. Manufacturers, however, were much more prone to be in favor of less restrictive practices, which would not invite retaliation that would interfere with their ability to export to the United States.[16] As we will see a few years later, the division of political actors along the lines of their economic interests would remain the same. British shipping and agricultural interests that benefited from the Orders in Council would press for their more stringent application in the face of American sanctions, while manufacturing interests would petition for their removal or relaxation. In December 1806, the United States and Great Britain signed a treaty that resolved some of the questions, but it did not address the issue of impressment of American seamen into the Royal Navy, which eventually led to the War of 1812. Finally, in 1807, the West Indian interests and their allies in shipping were able to get the British government to adopt a more severe policy towards neutral shipping.

Stephen and his parliamentary allies argued correctly in their assertion that the United States would not risk war over the neutral shipping issue, but the Americans did impose sanctions. In April 1806, the U. S. Congress passed an act forbidding the importation of British luxury items, and in December 1807 passed the Embargo Act, which ostensibly completely cut off U. S.-British trade.[17] However, smuggling via Canada and the constant stream of American ships (which were supposed to remain in port) slipping though the blockade on various pretexts detracted from the effectiveness of the Embargo Act.[18] Nonetheless, there was a serious reduction in the volume of trade between the United States and Great Britain.

The question that is examined here is: What were the political effects of this action in Britain? The Embargo was supposed to persuade the British to drop the Orders in Council, which restricted neutral shipping rights, but the British government seemed impervious to all

American attempts to influence it through economic channels, and the OIC remained rigidly in place until after the American government issued a de facto repeal of the Non-Importation act. This may have been because the U. S. was less able to withstand the pressure the embargo inflicted on its own economy and political system, but we must also look at the interests groups who benefited from the embargo in Great Britain and their activities. If those who gained from sanctions acted through their parliamentary representatives to maintain the Orders in Council, then sanctions may have been counterproductive since their intended effect was to force the removal of the OIC.

We would expect that exporters would be against the policies that prompted the sanctions while the producers of import-competing products would be in favor of these same policies. In this case the exporters were British manufacturers whereas the import-competing products were agricultural, and the division of opinion on the Orders in Council appears to fall neatly along these lines. One merchant banker criticized the Orders in Council arguing that they would harm Britain more than the U. S. in the long run. He noted that the United States took in, on average, £6,845,000 worth of British manufactured goods per year and that most of the American re-exports were to areas closed to British traders anyway. Other representatives of manufacturing interests deemed the Orders in Council as pointless and self-destructive, especially in such industrial centers as Liverpool. On the other hand, representatives from agricultural regions of Britain downplayed the effects of Orders in Council, or tried to present them in a positive light.

The American government replaced the embargo with the Non-Intercourse Act of March 1809. The result was that instead of keeping American ships in port, they were free to go to anywhere except British and French ports and buy British or French goods from other neutrals. The British were willing to ease the Orders in Council when the Americans announced that they would end the Non-Intercourse act with whichever of the two belligerents allowed freer neutral trade, but despite the work of the British minister to the United States, London was not willing to rescind the Orders in Council because certain conditions were not included in the agreement that he had come to with the American government. But in the interim before the British government had rejected the proposal, the temporary understanding reached by the British minister and the American government left American ports open to a virtual flood of British goods. The American embargo was more or less dead at this point, and the United States gave up on using economic means of persuading Great Britain to drop the Orders in Council in February 1811.[19]

Ironically, the British only maintained the Orders in Council until 1812. Up until then, they had been able to sublimate the demands of merchants that the OIC, be rescinded to the desire to successfully prosecute the war with France, but this changed when many South American investments went sour and Britain faced a serious economic depression. In an effort to revive the manufacturing sector, the OIC were repealed in 1812, and merchants rushed to fill orders bound for the United States.[20]

MANUFACTURING VERSUS AGRICULTURE IN THE HOUSE OF COMMONS

In March 1808, a group of merchants from London, Manchester, and Liverpool joined forces to petition Parliament for a reconsideration of the OIC, which had ruined trade with the United States.[21]   Mr. Alderman Combe of London presented the initial petition:

That the petitioners contemplate with the greatest anxiety and apprehension, the alarming consequences with which they are threatened from certain OIC, purporting to be issued "for the protection of the Trade and navigation of Great Britain" but on which they are induced, after mature consideration, to believe that they must be productive of the most ruinous effects. [22]

Mr. Shakspear Phillips of the Nathaniel and Faulkner Phillips and Company Trading House testified that "I should not think it likely that America would withdraw her embargo while the OIC continued," and that "I should apprehend those OIC would produce hostilities between this country and America," which was the stated reason for why he believed that he would not risk trade with the United States until the OIC were lifted. If the conflict broke out into open hostilities, there would be no guarantee of payments, which at the time took between 12 and 18 months to collect. In addition, he feared (correctly so) that Great Britain was soon to feel the strains of the reduced trade. Because of this and his fellow merchants' inability to export goods "for fear of a rupture taking place between the two countries, there has been a great reduction in the value of goods resulting from the oversupply because of the loss of the American market."[23]

George Palmer of the merchant house John Guest and Company took the floor to declare that the reluctance to engage in trade with the United States was universal and that "I know the great majority of houses will not ship a single package."[24] But if the Orders in Council were revoked, they would undoubtedly resume shipments. Likewise, William Bell of William and John Bell and Company concurred that the problem was not in Washington but in Whitehall. "If the U. S. embargo was removed but OIC stayed we would not ship because without the market of the continent they would never be able to pay us."[25]

These merchants and traders found sympathetic MPs in the House of Commons who rose to support them. Windham asked sarcastically, "We might it seems be able to starve the continent and still not be affected ourselves. What! starve the continent and not be affected ourselves! was this then the manner in which these vigorous measures were to effectuate the salvation of the country?"[26] Sir Arthur Piggott raised the specter of unemployment and the social unrest that accompanies it, noting that "were there not thousands of manufacturers at this moment without employment or with only half employment?"[27] Mr. Whitbread tried to explain the importance of friendly relations with the United States: "It must appear that cordially united with her (America), we might together cope with the living world were it against us; and with the exception of America, might I say that the living world is against us!"[28] It is worth noting that two of these MPs, Piggott and Whitbread, came from relatively industrial areas in Surrey.

These merchants and their parliamentary allies clearly understood that the source of their problems lay in Westminster and not in America, and their reaction was exactly what the United States desired. The intention of the sanctions against Britain was to cause enough economic damage that influential groups would petition the British government to revoke the OIC, and this is precisely what happened. A group of no less than 30 merchants representing some of the largest firms of the day petitioned and testified before the House of Commons with the intention of having the OIC revoked, which would serve their interests as well as America's. They were, however, quite unsuccessful in this endeavor, and why they failed reveals that the often counterproductive effects of sanctions are not restricted to the twentieth century.

One explanation for their lack of success in swaying Parliament to act in their interest is that national security concerns took precedence over the prosperity of a few merchants. This is possible, and it was certainly used as a pretext by those who supported the more rigorous enforcement of the OIC, but it does not stand up to serious examination. At the same time as this debate was occurring in Great Britain, France was implementing the Continental System through a series of decrees (most notably the Berlin and Milan decrees), which were designed to impoverish Britain by cutting it off from its export markets in continental Europe. The other intended effect of the Continental System was to develop indigenous industries on the continent that would free it from dependence on British industry and commerce. The OIC that were responsible for destroying trade with the United States only intensified the negative effects of the Continental System and made matters considerably worse for Britain and British interests on the whole. Denied access to continental markets, British manufacturers and traders needed other export markets such as the United States even more than before. Without them, the British economy and in fact British society was in jeopardy since there were numerous violent protests resulting from the increased unemployment in the cities that the lack of export markets produced at this time.

On the other hand, if the United States and other neutrals were allowed to trade with enemy, the importation of goods could only hinder Napoleon's development strategy for the continent. Granted that the United States was incapable of manufacturing serious substitutes for many British products, but sympathetic American traders would no doubt be willing to relabel and transship goods.[29] Overall it seems that British national security interests could not serve as a valid justification for maintaining the OIC or that at the very least there is a persuasive argument that its national interests would be better served by freeing trade as much as possible.

The petitioners were obviously concerned that the interruption of trade with the United States would drive them out of business, and they took their case before Parliament in the hope that they could influence the British government's policy toward the United States. They understood that the OIC were directly responsible for the American Non-Intercourse Act and sought to have the OIC dropped or at least modified in order to mollify the Americans. Instead, Parliament actually intensified the OIC and the correspondence between the American envoy and George Canning reveal a distinctly provocative tone in the British pronouncements and refusals to even consider any conciliatory measures.[30] If a group of ostensibly powerful and influential merchants and manufacturers could not persuade Parliament to act in their interest, then we must consider the actions of an interest group on the other side of the issue powerful enough to override them and keep the OIC in place: British landowners.

Here we can turn to the division of interests that changing exposure to trade should produce. When the Corn Laws debate became a central issue 30 years later, this division was starkly revealed, with manufacturers forming the Anti-Corn Law League and landowners standing in firm opposition to any relaxation of the laws that guarded their interests. In other words, the owners and intensive users of relatively abundant factors who would benefit from free trade successfully exerted pressure on the political system to have the trade regime changed in their favor, while the owners of the relatively scarce factor, land, sought to prevent any increased exposure to international trade.

The model would predict the exact opposite situation with regard to the debate over the OIC, which by prompting an American embargo constrained Britain's exposure to international trade. This obviously hurt the owners of abundant factors, but it should have benefited the owners of the scarce resource. If we find evidence that the agricultural elite and their representatives in Parliament exerted pressure to maintain or strengthen the OIC, then sanctions in this case may have been directly counterproductive. By benefiting a small, but extremely powerful class, the American Non-Intercourse Act may have produced the exact opposite effect from what was desired. The intention was to force Britain to negate the OIC, but by increasing the profits of the agricultural elite, they may have, in fact, made matters worse for American interests.

Of all the debates on the Orders in Council, probably the most important was on March 6-7, 1809. The debate lasted through the night and the bill presented by Whitbread called for an end to the OIC. Whitbread gave a long and impassioned speech outlining the harmful effects that the OIC had on Great Britain, and accused the government of issuing deliberately misleading statements regarding their effects, which claimed they benefited manufacturers who would be the benefactors of a monopoly on raw materials. The government itself would be the recipient of increase revenues from transit duties, and in strategic terms, the OIC would deprive the continent of products and subdue Napoleon's ability to expand further.

However, according to Whitbread, what actually happened was a diminution of imports and exports totaling 11 million pounds.

From America previous to these orders (in council), Great Britain imported of cotton wool 32 million pounds. Since that part of the world was closed against our commerce, what has been our supply of that article? Why sir, from Asia and the Portuguese settlements in South America, we imported 5 millions. Thus the illustration which this system afford both the total command of raw materials for our manufactures is by furnishing us with a deficit of 27 millions of pounds.[31]

In addition, the manufacturing slowdown had serious social consequences, especially in Manchester, "where the poor rates have risen from 24,000 to 49,000 in consequence of the number of manufacturers thrown out of bread; where of the numerous cotton mills which were formerly employed, 32 are now idle and six only at work." These effects were not limited to England. The lack of American flax seed imports was also destroying the Irish linen industry.

Whitbread also pointed to the existence of profiteers, although was polite enough not to accuse his colleagues from agricultural regions directly. "I do admit that by such a system some will be found obtaining a profit even from the general calamity, in the same manner as we know that by the late conflagrations, though many are thrown out of bread and employment, others are receiving from the very occurrence support and additional earnings." While not naming the profiteers, Whitbread was clearly alluding to the fact that sectors in direct competition with American imports were gaining from the trade disruption. [32]

Despite Whitbread's reasoned petition for the removal of the Orders in Council, the House of Commons was not swayed and a sizable majority agreed with the response offered by Stephens. "It might be asked what have we gained by the Orders in Council," asks Stephens rhetorically. "To which he would answer, all that we have not lost. In this way, the question was not how much our trade has encreased (sic) under the operation of the Orders in Council, but that in reality all that we had; all that was now left to us was owing to them. He was astonished to hear it contended that through our Orders in Council, we had lost the trade of America. The Non-Importation act and the Embargo, and not our Orders in Council had excluded us from this trade."[33] Stephens went on to express his indignance at the American response to Britain's actions in an attempt to pin the blame on America for whatever ills had befallen Britain. "Nothing could equal the insolence practiced towards us by a power, who while she could not shew (sic) a single flag on the ocean, dared to declare the ports of so superior a maritime power in a state of blockade. Such an insult and the evils it was calculated to produce, we were warranted by the law of nations in resenting, and also in retaliating."[34]

So far we have focused exclusively on the House of Commons, which ignores the other major legislative body of Great Britain: the House of Lords. While the House of Lords debates are interesting, ultimately they will not reveal much for the purposes of this study. The Lords are by definition landowners and as such they should all be in favor of anything that protects agriculture. Some Lords were opposed to the Orders in Council but that may have been because they were invested heavily in manufacturing or overseas trade in some manner, or it may have just been their ideological position regardless of their immediate self-interest. Also the Lords do not represent anyone but themselves and as such are not beholden to represent the interests of the region from which they come. Therefore, short of conducting detailed studies of where each member of the House of Lords derived his income, where individual members of the House of Lords stood on the Orders in Council will not yield any statistically viable data.

Even so, it is interesting to note that several Lords were very much opposed to the Orders in Council. Lord Auckland went so far as to rise and declare that "he professed to God, that he was still totally unable to ascertain their nature or drift, much less to divine the remotest possibility of interest or advantage likely to accrue to this country from their adoption. Such conduct could only be compared to the insanity of maniacs." [35] Likewise, Lord Grenville stood out as one of the most vocal opponents in the aristocracy. "It could not be supposed that it was the object of those who framed them (the OIC) totally to destroy the commerce of this country," stated Grenville, "And yet, on reading over the Orders it would be difficult to discover that any other effect could be produced from them than the total destruction of that commerce." [36] Grenville also went to great lengths to convince his fellow Lords that the they could not afford to alienate the United States, stating that he "laboured under the melancholy conviction that the consequences of hostility would be extremely detrimental to both.. We had already all Europe against us: we should not be too eager to add America to the long and formidable catalogue of our enemies." [37]

Other Lords attacked the Orders in Council on legal grounds, arguing that Great Britain did not have a moral or legal right to impose such restrictions on neutral shipping. "Contrary to the law of nations and the law of the land. The OIC of 7th January last year was in retaliation for a Decree of the French Government," stated Lord Petty. "Nothing therefore, could justify us in retaliating upon America an act of hostility, which was directed by our enemy, not against neutrals, but against us--his opponents in this contest." [38] Lord Erskine was also opposed on the same grounds. "It is a new application of the term retaliation," said Erskine, "that if A strikes me, I may retaliate by striking B. Here the phrase cannot apply either in grammar, common sense or justice." [39]

Despite these objections, the majority of the House of Lords was consistently in favor of the Orders in Council and their strict application. Cabinet officials such as Home Secretary Lord Hawksbury were especially insistent that Great Britain not curry the favor of their American cousins by "the surrender of any of our rights, much less of our maritime rights, upon which our very existence might be said to depend." [40] Spencer Perceval, Chancellor of the Exchequer, maintained that "we had a complete right to retaliate upon the enemy their own measures; that if the enemy declared we should have no trade; we had a right to declare that they should have no trade." [41] Despite the fact that Grenville and others correctly surmised that the Orders in

Council would set Great Britain on the path to war with the United States, Perceval asserted that "Some persons apprehended that they (the Orders in Council) might induce America to go to war with us. He trusted not; he believed not."[42]   "It was impossible that the Americans could look at the OIC without perceiving in them any instances of caution not to injure America. There were various exceptions in diminution of the effect of those Orders which showed that we were desirous of doing as little injury to America as possible."[43]   Despite the claims, there is no indication that the British government did anything to moderate the effects of its policies regarding neutral shipping rights. Quite the contrary, there is every indication in the correspondence between Foreign Secretary Canning and his American counterparts that the British government understood how the Orders in Council were affecting the United States and still took measures to intensify them.

TESTING THE MODEL: AGRICULTURE VERSUS MANUFACTURING IN THE HOUSE OF COMMONS

The model would predict that MPs from rural districts representing the interests of landowners would be in favor of the OIC, while MPs from urban districts representing the interests of manufacturing would be opposed. Ideally, we would be able to look at the voting patterns of the individual members of the House of Commons and determine if those from more rural districts tended to be in favor of the Orders in Council than their urban counterparts, indicating the sort of urban/rural cleavage we would expect on trade-related issues given the relative factor endowments of Great Britain. Unfortunately, the House of Commons did not begin to keep accurate lists of how individual Members of Parliament voted (Division Lists) until the late 1830s. Therefore, it was necessary to approximate how individual members would have voted based on their comments in parliamentary debates preceding the votes. Presumably, members who spoke either in favor of or against the Orders in Council voted that way, so by combing the records of the debates, we can construct a sample against which to test the hypothesis.

The 1811 census of Great Britain provides the means of determining whether an MP was from a rural or urban district.[44] The census contains data for parish, township, and county, including the number of households involved in either agriculture or manufacturing. By taking a simple ratio of agricultural households divided by manufacturing households, we have a reasonable indicator of how industrialized a given region was in 1811 (see Table 3.1). Those with the highest ratios are the most heavily involved in agriculture and, presumably, have the most to gain from restricted trade with the United States, as well as the most to lose from a liberalization of that trade.

We can now match the individual MPs to their respective counties to determine how good a predictor the agriculture/manufacturing ratio is for where an MP stood on the Orders in Council. One flaw in this strategy is that the county is a fairly large area and may contain both areas with high and low agriculture/manufacturing ratios. Generally speaking, this is not a major problem in early nineteenth-century England since industry was still quite concentrated, but in order to minimize its distorting effects, data for the township, city, or parish the MP represents is used whenever available.

Twenty-six Members of Parliament are on record as having spoken clearly in favor or against the Orders in Council, or in some cases, are recorded as having voted on the issue (see Table 3.2). There is a close correlation between the agriculture/manufacturing ratio of the region the individual MP represents and where he stood on the OIC, which demonstrates that sanctions were highly counterproductive in this instance and helps to explain why the sanctions were ineffective despite their economic impact. The Non-Importation Act of 1807 and subsequent American sanctions had the desired effect economically, but failed politically because the merchants and manufacturers harmed by these measures were not as powerful as the landed interests who benefited from the reduction in trade between the United States and Great Britain. Thirty years later, the situation had changed drastically and manufacturing interests were able to put an end to the Corn Laws, but in the period 1807-1811, they simply could not prevail in a contest that pitted the interests of agriculture against the interests of export-oriented manufacturers.

MPs who spoke in favor of the OIC came from districts where families who derived their income from manufacturing were outnumbered by families who derived their income from agriculture by a margin of more than 2 to 1. In contrast, MPs who stood opposed to the OIC hailed from regions where on average manufacturing families outnumbered agricultural families by more than 1.5 to 1. This is not to say that Britain was a perfectly representative democracy in the early nineteenth century, but we can safely assume that a region in which most families derive their incomes from agriculture, the elites who enjoy the right to vote, will very likely derive much of their income from agriculture as well, and vice versa for more industrial regions.

Table 3. 1
Comparison of Number of Families Employed in Agriculture to Number of Families Employed in Manufacturing in 1811 (by County)

COUNTY	AG. FAMILIES	MFG. FAMILIES	AG/MFG RATIO
Bedford	9,431	4,155	2.27
Berks	13,409	7,584	1.77
Buckingham	13,993	8,424	1.66
Cambridge	12,831	5,303	2.42
Chester	16,396	23,043	0.71
Cumberland	10,868	11,448	0.95
Cornwall	17,465	10,954	1.59
Derby	14,283	15,825	0.90
Devon	33,044	30,977	1.07
Dorset	12,982	9,607	1.35
Durham	10,288	17,094	0.60
Essex	28,517	14,182	2.01
Gloucester	20,782	29,988	0.69
Hereford	12,599	5,044	2.50
Hertford	11,998	7,192	1.67
Huntingdon	5,361	2,205	2.43
Kent	27,077	27,996	0.97
Lancaster	23,305	114,522	0.20
Leicester	11,700	17,027	0.69
Lincoln	29,881	13,184	2.27
Middlesex	9,088	135,398	0.07
Monmouth	5,815	4,812	1.21
Norfolk	31,454	23,082	1.36
Northampton	15,235	3,525	4.32
Nottingham	12,293	18,928	0.65
Nrthumberland	10,945	16,547	0.66
Oxford	13,646	7,655	1.78
Rutland	2,025	1,028	1.97
Salop	16,693	16,744	1.00
Somerset	27,472	23,732	1.16
Southampton	21,401	18,024	1.19
Stafford	18,361	34,011	0.54
Suffolk	26,406	15,180	1.74
Surrey	12,417	35,160	0.35
Sussex	19,778	10,754	1.84
Warwick	15,131	29,775	0.51
Westmorland	4,613	2,870	1.61
Wilts	22,657	14,857	1.53

Worcester	13,818	16,865	0.82
York, East	14,517	12,926	1.12
York, North	16,570	19,864	0.83
York, West.	30,868	86,522	0.36

Source :1811 Census records drawn *from Abstract of the Answers and Returns Made pursuant to An Act for Taking an Account of the Population of Great Britain and of the Increse or Diminution thereof.*

Table 3. 2
Ag/Mfg Ratio and Parliamentary Position on OIC

MP	REGION	AG/MFG RATIO	OIC POSITION	MEAN AG/MFG
Combe	London	0	opposed	0.67
Gascoyne	Liverpool	0.01	opposed	
Smith	Norwich	0.05	opposed	
Horner	Middlesex	0.07	opposed	
Dundas	Richmond, York	0.31	opposed	
Leman	Penryn, Crnwall.	0.32	opposed	
Whitbread	Reidford, Surrey	0.36	opposed	
Abercromby	Midhurst, Surrey	0.36	opposed	
Piggot	Arundel, Sussex	0.56	opposed	
Greenhill	York	0.83	opposed	
Colborne	Cumbria	0.95	opposed	
Baring	Taunton, Smrset.	1.15	opposed	
Eden	Woodst Oxfrd.	1.78	opposed	
Pelham	Lincolnshire	2.67	opposed	
Shaw	London	0	for	2.24
Rose	Southhampton	1.18	for	
Wallace	Shaftsbury	1.35	for	
Bourne	Dorset	1.35	for	
Creevey	Norfolk	1.36	for	
Long	Wiltshire	1.53	for	
Hibbet	Sussex	1.84	for	
Canning	Hastings, Sussex	1.94	for	
Huchkisson	Essex	2.01	for	
Peele	Tamworth, Staff.	4.13	for	
Perceval	Northampton	4.32	for	
Stephens	St.Ives, Crnwall.	5.86	for	

Source: House of Commons Parliamentary Papers 1801-1900, 1811 census records

A chi-squared test to determine how close the actual distribution between two populations is to the predicted value reveals that the re-sults are highly significant. Here the median AG/MFG ratio was used to break the sample of 26 MPs into two groups of 13: A low AG/MFG group and a high AG/MFG group. The model predicts that the low AG/MFG group will be against the OIC and the High AG/MFG group will be in favor. Indeed, 92% of the MPs in the low group were against the OIC, and 85% of the MPs in the high group were in favor. The chances of such a distribution occurring randomly are less than 1 in 1,000.

$$x^2 = 15.48, \ p < .0001$$

	Against OIC	For OIC
Low AG/MFG Districts	12	1
High AG/MFG Districts	2	11

CONCLUSION

While this approach explains why the OIC were maintained in the face of American sanctions, it does not appear to explain why they were lifted in 1811. If the landed interests benefited from the sanctions and controlled the reigns of power to the degree that they could successfully override the interests of capital, why were they suddenly more conciliatory toward the United States a few years later? The answer is twofold. First, as was mentioned earlier, Great Britain was experiencing a severe economic depression as a result of the crash of the South American investment market, which had absorbed some of what would have gone to North America if sanctions had not been in place. This made the renewal of decent relations with the United States all the more important. Second, and more important, landed interests had ceased to gain from the American sanctions. Because of unusually bad weather, 1811 was a disastrous harvest year (see Figure 3.2). Great Britain could not feed itself, and in the absence of Baltic wheat imports eliminated by the continental system, it simply needed American grain imports.[45] These factors conspired to weaken the case of those who stood to gain from the Orders in Council while strengthening the position of those interests most harmed by them. Even so, the British attitude and actions toward its former colony changed only marginally. The agreement that contained enough concessions to persuade the Americans to drop the embargo was never ratified in Great Britain, and similar issues to those that prompted sanctions brought the two countries to war only a year later.

Figure 3. 2
Wheat Production in Britain 1807-1811

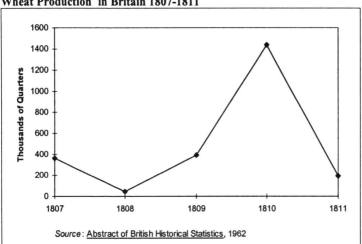

Source: Abstract of British Historical Statistics, 1962

Despite the national security rhetoric, which suffused the debate over the Orders in Council, basic economic self-interest was at the heart of the matter. Agricultural producers were able to capture rents in the form of higher grain prices in the absence of American imports and sought, through their parliamentary representatives, to keep the source of their protection in place for as long as possible. Only when American wheat became critical to British survival did Parliament consider making conciliatory gestures to America regarding neutral shipping rights.

This case provides an interesting test of the analytical framework employed in this study for several reasons. First, it demonstrates that the behavior the theory would predict under sanctions is not solely a modern phenomenon. Second, it offers some insight into when sanctions should be effective. Although this is a case in which sanctions clearly failed to achieve their stated aims, they certainly could have. The embargo would have soon been a very effective instrument for America if Britain had continued to have bad harvests and lack alternate suppliers. Britain would have had little choice but to accede to some American demands or risk its central security interests in Europe. Third, and most important, this case shows how sanctions can aid in the creation of an interest group that has a vested interest in seeing that sanctions, and the policies that prompted them, are maintained. While historical case studies such as this one may not be completely applicable to modern situations, they do demonstrate that the effects of trade-disrupting sanctions are not limited to the twentieth century.

NOTES

1. Frank E. Melvin, *Napoleon's Navigation System: A Study of Trade Control during the Continental Blockade* (New York: University of Pennsylvania, 1919), 191.

2. Cheryl Schoenhardt Bailey, *A Model of Trade Policy Liberalization looking inside the British Hegemon*, Ph.D. diss. (University of California Los Angeles, 1991).

3. Jeffrey Frankel, "The 1808-1809 Embargo of Britain," *Journal of Economic History* 42: no. 2 (1982): 291-302.

4. Eli Heckscher, *The Continental System: An Economic Interpretation* (Oxford: Clarendon Press, 1922), 38.

5. Melvin, *Napoleon's Navigation System*, 191.

6. Ibid., 93.

7. Andrew Kippis, *Considerations on the Provisional Treaty with America* (London, 1783), 33.

8. Ibid., 220.

9. John Baker Sheffield, *Observations on the Commerce of the American States* (London: 1783), 6.

10. Judith Blow Williams, *British Commercial Policy and Trade Expansion 1785-1850* (Oxford: Clarendon Press, 1972), 221.

11. Ibid., 224.

12. Frederick Eden, *Eight Letters on the Peace* (London, 1802), 85.

13. Judith Blow Williams notes that "except for the brief period from 1786-1793, when the two countries tried the interesting experiment of reciprocal trade with low duties and a minimum of restrictions, an experiment which it was hoped would be epoch-making, the keys to commercial relations between France and Great Britain were war, political hostility and economic rivalry." Williams, pp.186-7.

14. James Stephen, *War in Disguise* (London, 1805), 207-8.

15. Williams, 229.

16. Alexander Baring, *An Inquiry into the Causes and Consequences of the Orders in Council* (London, 1808), 81-2.

17. Williams, 232.

18. One notorious loophole in the embargo was the clause that allowed American ships to sail to foreign ports in order to collect the possessions of American citizens. This clause was so abused early in the embargo that Congress was forced to remove it from a subsequent version passed in 1809.

19. Williams, 234-5.

20. Ibid. This reconciliation was only temporary, as the two countries were at war before the year was out. It is interesting to note that one of the main by-products of the trade conflict between the United States and Britain was the development of new industries in the U. S. designed to fill the demand for manufactured goods that had formerly come from Britain. In terms of long-

time consequences detrimental to British exports, the most serious result of the embargo was the stimulus to American manufactures. "Shortages of British goods led to the growth of American industry not only in the east but also as far inland as Cincinnati, Ohio" (Williams, p. 236). This is essentially the mirror image of what occurred in Great Britain during the same time period. Land was the scarce resource in Great Britain and, as we will see, owners of that resource successfully constrained trade to their benefit. Likewise, capital and labor were in relatively short supply in the United States, so a trade disruption should have been in their best interests. If the scope of this chapter could be expanded, we would most likely find that these manufacturers who benefited from the embargo attempted to use their influence to ensure that the embargo stayed in place as long as possible.

21. Peter Cockton, ed., *House of Commons Parliamentary Papers 1801-1900*, vol. X (Cambridge: Chadwick-Healey, 1987), 85.

22. Ibid., 1056.

23. Ibid., 94-5.

24. Ibid.

25. Ibid., 214.

26. Ibid., 338.

27. Cockton, vol. XII, 1062.

28. Ibid., 1163.

29. The Continental System inspired very creative smuggling measures as Eli Hecksher elaborates on in *The Continental System*. The relabeling of goods was a common method of sneaking British goods into French-held territory. Hecksher tells the story of a British cloth manufacturer who at the time was making bolts of cloth with the label of a Sedan cloth manufacturer.

30. I am not the first to note the seemingly deliberately provocative character of Anglo-American official correspondence. Hecksher notes that rather than modify the Orders in Council in order to reach a mutually satisfactory agreement with the United States, "On the contrary, Canning, as foreign secretary, conducted the almost continuous exchange of notes with an ironic superiority and a diplomatic skill which were calculated to irritate more and more the American with its clumsier methods"(Hecksher, p.135) .

31. T. C. Hansard, *The Parliamentary Debates from the Year 1803 to the Present Time* (London: Longman Hurst, 1812), 1167. The records of the speeches made in the House of Commons are often recorded in the third person. Unless otherwise noted, when the word "he" is used, it refers to the speaker.

32. Ibid., 1168.

33. Ibid., 1187.

34. Ibid., 1188.

35. Hansard, vol. X, 150-1.

36. Ibid., 153.

37. Ibid., 312.

38. Ibid., 315-318.

39. Ibid., 938.

40. Ibid., 312-13.

41. Ibid., 324.

42. Ibid., 329.

43. Ibid.

44. 1811 Census records drawn from *Abstract of the Answers and Returns Made pursuant to An Act for Taking an Account of the Population of Great Britain and of the Increse or Diminution thereof* (London: House of Commons, 1812).

45. A. Gayer, W. Rostow, and A. Swartz, *Growth and Fluctuation of the British Economy*, vol. 1 (London: Barnes and Noble, 1953), 84. The grain trade between the continent and Britain flowed relatively freely during the war, but in 1810 France was confronted with shortages and blocked the export of all grain. Later that year, some grain shipments were allowed.

4

Sanctions Against Yugoslavia

Yugoslavia was one of the brighter points in Eastern Europe through-out the Cold War. Neither of the Warsaw Pact nor in the western camp, Marshal Josef Broz Tito drove the multiethnic federation down a path that seemed to lead to relative independence and prosperity. In 1991, however, Tito's Yugoslavia collapsed into a frenzy of ethnic warfare so intense it prompted comparisons with the Holocaust. Pent up resent-ments stretching back hundreds of years surfaced and sparked violence between Serbs, Croats, and Muslims, who for the past 50 years had been known to the outside world simply as "Yugoslavians." The scenes played out in Srebenica, Vukovar, and Sarajevo made it all too clear how fragile and artificial that identity was.

The international community responded with a mixed basket of tools to put an end to the worst fighting Europe had seen since World War II. Diplomatic efforts such as the Vance-Owen plan attempted to find the perfect balance of territory that would satisfy the interests of all the ethnicities. When diplomacy failed, NATO air strikes helped to equalize the balance of power and bring parties back to the negotiating table. A key part of the international response, however, was economic sanctions.

But what was the effect of economic sanctions on the Yugoslavian conflict? It is not enough to say that sanctions ultimately "worked" because they helped bring about the Dayton Accords (which appeared to bring the conflict to a managed state as long as Western military power could enforce the peace). Nor is it sufficient to dismiss sanctions altogether, because they did not force an end to the violence by themselves. Rather, a more nuanced approach is warranted. Some of the sanctions, particularly the financial variant, were quite effective and feared by the Yugoslavian government. However, sanctions that constrained the flow of goods, especially oil, fueled the rise of a powerful criminal/paramilitary element that became politically active to ensure that the source of its income, namely sanctions, was not removed.

Financial sanctions were particularly feared by Slobodan Milosevic, president of the Yugoslavian Federation. The threat of cutting off Serbia's access to international capital weighed heavily on Milosevic and may have been an important factor that drove him to sign the Vance-Owen plan dividing Bosnia into a group of autonomous cantons. "He [Milosevic] did not want financial sanctions," said Lord Owen, co-author of the plan. "We should have imposed financial sanctions months, even years ago."[1]

If we measure the effectiveness of sanctions in terms of the actual damage they cause to the economy, then sanctions have definitely been effective. GDP plummeted in 1992 and only began to recover in 1995. The per capita GDP dropped from almost $2,670 in 1991 to $1,273 in 1993. By 1995, the recovery had only inched its way back to just over $1,500.[2]

Sanctions clearly had severe negative effects on the economy over time in the larger sense, but this is not the same as effective sanctions. We must keep in mind the power that small groups, which gain from any economic distortion, may have over the interests of the country as a whole. In this case, the main profiteers were the individuals who controlled the gasoline smuggling trade, which established firm links to political organizations in the pursuit of their interests. In doing so, they were able to sever the link between economic pain and political change.

The theory of sanctions presented earlier suggests that export sanctions act as protective tariffs, thus benefiting the owners and intensive users of scarce resources. In many cases in this study (Yugoslavia included), the scarce resource is capital, which would lead us to assume that sanctions will result in import substitution industrialization (ISI), and that those who gain from the substitution process will engage in rent seeking to ensure that their protective shield stays in place. In the case of Yugoslavia, it is clear that there has been some ISI, but pervasive smuggling eliminates much of the demand for domestically produced import substitutes. This leads us to an important corollary: If the sanctioned goods can be supplied through other means for less than what it would cost to manufacture domestic substitutes, then those who profit from the illegal trade will engage in rent seeking.

This is an important point to keep in mind because just as import substitute manufacturers have an incentive to support the parties responsible for sanctions, so do individuals engaged in non-manufacturing activities that benefit from export sanctions. In the case of these individuals, the incentive to keep sanctions in place is even greater because while manufacturers could simply return to the level and type of output they were at before sanctions, smugglers and black marketers would have no demand for their services once sanctions are removed.

Sanctions have had an impact on the Serbian economy, but it is difficult to determine how much of the dire economic situation is owed to them rather than simply to the continuing economic decline of the region since the breakup of the Yugoslavian federation. The United Nations did not impose mandatory sanctions until May 1992, and the Yugoslavian economy was in a tailspin long before then. Industrial production fell 25% in 1993 from the previous year, on top of an 18% decrease in 1991. Although the agricultural sector has performed better than the industrial sector, it has lost ground as well, showing a decline of 18% in 1992 and a comparatively small 7% decline in 1993. In addition, hyperinflation (which was only brought under control in the spring of 1994) seriously eroded purchasing power. Real salaries fell almost 49% in 1992 and an additional 61% in 1993.[3] Clearly economic conditions have worsened severely since the imposition of sanctions, but it is not clear if these aggregate figures reflect anything more than the continuing decline of the Yugoslavian economy, a trend that began long before the international community decided to punish the country with economic sanctions.

Nonetheless, it can be argued that sanctions contributed to this decline by triggering hyperinflation and severe shortages. Until the 1994 stabilization program, crippling six-digit inflation wiped out many citizens' savings and forced those on fixed incomes to rely on charity. The sanctions-induced fuel shortage contributed to unemployment and higher prices for many items, which should have caused enough popular discontent to force Serbian compliance with UN resolutions. Instead, Serbia maintained its direction until threatened with NATO military force, a fact that poses a puzzle that cannot be explained in purely economic terms.

It should be noted that not every sector of the economy is as hard hit as the aggregate figures for industrial and agricultural production would suggest. Petroleum production has slowly but steadily increased to partially fill in the gap between supply and demand created by sanctions. Although much of the gasoline used in Serbia is smuggled across the Romanian border or is illegally transported down the Danube river,

Serbia is capable of providing for approximately one-third of its needs, and that sector of the economy appears to be flourishing.

In addition, the aggregate figures for employment and electrical consumption do not correlate with the strong declines in the industrial sector. For example, while employment drops precipitously during the sanctions period according to official aggregate figures, it increases in certain areas such as "workers in private shops." At the same time we would expect to see a drop in electrical generation and consumption proportional in size to the decline of Serbian industry, but while the official figures for industrial production fall 25% from 1992 to 1993, electrical generation only falls 8% in the same period.

This could be a reflection of the relatively low proportion of electricity consumed by industry, but it also may be an indication of the Yugoslavian government's desire to portray the impact of sanctions on the economy as greater than it actually is in order to garner sympathy and possibly relief from the international pressure it currently experiences. The executive summary of the *1993 Basic Data on Socio-Economic Movements* depicts a country severely weakened by sanctions, and other official statements reveal the image that the government wishes to project. Foreign Minister Vladislav Jovanovic appealed for the lifting of sanctions in May 1992, claiming they were "unjust and genocidal."[4]   A letter from a organization of pro-Milosevic Yugoslavian medical doctors to the United Nations claims that the trade sanctions have cost thousands of lives and must be lifted. The doctors blame critical shortages of medical supplies on sanctions, even though these items are not blocked under the terms of the UN resolutions, and most shortages were reportedly the result of hospital personnel selling supplies on the black market. The government clearly finds some utility in portraying the country as more severely affected by sanctions than it is and works through official and unofficial channels to create this image.

ALTERNATIVE EXPLANATIONS: ANCIENT HATREDS OR MODERN CAUSES?

The are three facets to the conventional wisdom regarding the effect of sanctions on Yugoslavia and why they have not achieved their stated goals. First, sanctions were ineffective because the ancient ethnic hatreds driving the conflict are so deep that external pressure is of little relevance to the antagonists. Second, through extensive control of the media, the government was able to twist sanctions to its benefit. Third, sanctions are a classic case of too little too late, and their effect was blunted by poor implementation. All of these points are valid to some degree, but they cannot explain why support for the nationalist parties whose actions brought about sanctions has increased when sanctions are at least partially responsible for Serbia's high inflation, high unemployment, absurdly low wages, and other economic miseries.[5]

One of the most popular explanations of the Yugoslavian conflict is that "ancient ethnic hatreds" drive the conflict between Serbs, Croats, and Moslems. During the 500 year-long Turkish occupation, the Ottoman Empire used Moslem converts to suppress their Christian counterparts in the region, creating a source of tension that is still felt in the Balkans. With a history of occupation by the Austro-Hungarian and Ottoman empires and situated on the battle-scarred border between the Christian and Muslim worlds, the Balkan peoples have had leading roles in some of the bloodiest conflicts in European history. The most famous example is of course World War I, triggered by the assassination of Austrian Archduke Franz Ferdinand by a Serbian patriot in a bid to further Serbia's claim to Bosnia, a claim that Serbia still holds dear.

Proponents of the ancient hatreds thesis argue that these ethnic tensions were never far from the surface, and once the communist suppression of ethnic expression was lifted, people simply returned to their deeply ingrained ways.[6] "Don't forget that this was all part of Croatia in 1101," says a Croatian soldier in Mostar, seemingly unaware that Croatia did not exist in any coherent form nine hundred years ago. "Muslims and Serbs took it away from us."[7] Others point to the seemingly irrational behavior of the combatants and conclude the conflict is simply beyond understanding. "This is the Balkans-rationality isn't a reliable compass," observes a Western diplomat in Belgrade. "All through this conflict, we've seen people who have recognized the disaster ahead and plunged forward anyway."[8] The popular perception, at least in the United States, is that the conflict is deeply rooted in the history of the region and is beyond an easily negotiated resolution.

Much of the conflict, however, can be traced to more recent events that made cooperation between these ethnic groups unlikely after the collapse of Tito's Yugoslavia. The main conflict historically has been between Serbs and Croats. Serbs dominate the region and have had aspirations of a "Greater Serbia" at least since the early part of this century. Croats, on the other hand, believe that the postwar Yugoslavian federation sapped them of resources and was disproportionately dominated by Serbs. There is some empirical evidence to support the Croatian perspective. Croatia was the industrial center of the region before World War II but was afterwards gradually drained financially and industrially in favor of Serbia and Bosnia. Industry accounted for 33% of Croatia's GDP in 1925, but by 1971 that figure had dropped to 18%. In addition, new investments and upgrading of existing infrastructure were heavily concentrated in other parts of the Yugoslavian Federation at the expense of Croatia. Croatian ports, for example, accounted for more than 80% of the total Yugoslavian maritime traffic but received barely 40% of the funds allocated for port modernization during the time of the federation.[9]

Croats also point to the disproportionate role that Serbs played in the political and military leadership of Yugoslavia. Despite the fact that Croats were a major part of the guerrilla force that liberated the region from Nazi control in World War II, Croats made up only 15% of the officer corps of the Yugoslav People's Army by 1980. In civil service employment, Croats appear to be at a distinct disadvantage as well. While Serbs, who are approximately 42% of the population, account for nearly 74% of the Federal Administration in 1978, Croats occupied a mere 6% even though they are nearly 22% of the total population of Yugoslavia. Croats also claim the Yugoslavian Federation deprived them of political representation. Croatia had a Serbian population of only 14% during Tito's reign, but the Croatian communist leadership was always disproportionately Serbian and consistently featured at least one Serb among its two or three representatives in the Federal Presidency.[10] To many Croats, the Federal Republic of Yugoslavia was a less than equal partnership in which they were in constant danger of being overwhelmed by the Serbian plurality.

Needless to say, Serbs have a markedly different view of the conflict. From their point of view, the only way that region could ever be peaceful, stable, and ensure the safety of Serbs who live in regions outside of Serbia proper, is to build an expanded "Greater Serbia." Serbs are the only ethnic group to have ever had a state in the region; Slovenia, Croatia, and Bosnia were under either Ottoman or Austro-Hungarian domination until the creation of Yugoslavia after World War I. The Yugoslav idea has always been centered around Belgrade, and even in the days of the Federal Republic, Serbia always dominated and must continue to do so. Without Serbian regional hegemony, ask many Serbs, who will protect ethnic Serbs in Bosnia, Croatia, and other remnants of Yugoslavia? Serbs remember all too well the savagery of the Nazi-backed Croatian fascist regime during World War II, which slaughtered 700,000 Serbs, Gypsies, and Jews and see the conflict as a defensive battle against Bosnian Muslims and Croatians. Given the history of the Balkans, they believe that they are the only real nation-state in the region and their leadership is the key to regional stability. At the same time, they have historically justified concerns for the safety of ethnic Serbs who live in areas not under direct Serbian control.[11]

There is a widespread perception among Serbs that they are in fact on the defensive, protecting themselves from what amounts to a second coming of the Islamic legions. In market stalls around Belgrade, pamphlets and books detailing the allegedly aggressive intentions of the Bosnian Republic's President Itzabegavic can be purchased. Texts detailing the unfair treatment the country has suffered at the hands of the Western powers in the face of Moslem aggression fill bookstore windows. One such book, entitled *A Dictionary of Misconceptions* (available in both Serbo-Croatian and English from the Serbian Ministry of Information), exemplifies this sort of literature:

It is not true that the Moslems are "unarmed" victims. In reality they have strong motives for continuing a war of conquest, and certainly do not need international protection. They merely need to mask their military assets in order to secure an advantage against the others and easily acquire a strong, unitary Islamic state.[12]

Whether justified or not, many Serbs are clearly concerned that their ethnicity's survival would be in jeopardy if they do not proceed with the policies that brought sanctions to bear against Yugoslavia.

Although there is considerable evidence to support the idea that the Balkan conflict is driven by both ancient and modern ethnic hatreds, many observers dismiss this, pointing to the decreasing importance of ethnicity in the region since World War II. Before the breakup of the Federal Republic, many citizens believed that they were "Yugoslavian" rather than Serbian or Croatian, and intermarriage was so commonplace in the postwar period that it became very difficult to determine a particular individual's ethnic heritage. Given this, it seems strange that these long-buried conflicts should suddenly rise to the surface. But according to Vladimir Matic, former Yugoslavian Deputy Foreign Minister, the reemergence of ethnic conflict is the result of the policies of the federal government in the 1960s and 1970s, designed to reinvigorate Yugoslavia's economy. In an attempt to get away from inefficient centralized industries, Yugoslavia began to spread its industrial base around the country, and as a consequence, each region began to believe that independence was a viable alternative.[13] Other accounts support Matic's position, most of which trace the demise of Yugoslavia to the 1974 constitution under which Yugoslavia became a "de facto confederation. Under this Constitution--the most flawed aspect of Tito's legacy--all real power was devolved into the hands of the LCYs

(League of Communists of Yugoslavia) tribal chieftains in the country's six republics and two autonomous provinces."[14]

The ensuing weakness of the federal government created a system whereby, "the retention and protection of regional power bases and interests took priority over consideration of national unity."[15] It soon became apparent to many economists that the Yugoslavian ideal was doomed. "The Yugoslav economy has disintegrated and has evolved from a unified economy and market into eight autarchic national economies and markets," writes Ivo Bicanic in 1988. "This has prevented the emergence of a consensus around an all-Yugoslav economic policy which might efficiently solve the current economic crisis."[16] In short, in its attempt to stimulate the flagging economy, the federal government inadvertently weakened the Yugoslavian ideal and fostered the idea that each republic could function as an independent entity.

Another often cited reason for the failure of sanctions is that the government controls the media and can shift blame for the country's economic woes to external actors. Through extensive state control of the media, President Milosevic has been able to project an image of an encircled Serbia fighting for its survival against a hostile coalition of international enemies. By pinning all responsibility for Serbia's woes on the West, Milosevic is able to rally voters to his cause because, in the words of one Serbian citizen as he cast his vote for Milosevic, he "believed it would most irk his Western enemies. Milosevic is the best man to get sanctions lifted."[17]

While there is some limited opposition press, it can be severely constrained almost at Milosevic's whim. Many opposition journals face harassment and restrictions. The weekly opposition magazine *Vreme* can usually only be purchased from its staff who sell it in the street, unable as they are to get newsstands to carry the magazine. The most important opposition newspaper, *Borba*, was effectively shut down in December 1994 when the government refused to renew its private enterprise license and, to make matters worse, began to issue a propaganda-filled paper under the same name. Before sanctions, most major newsstands carried *Time*, *Newsweek*, *The Wall Street Journal Europe*, *The Economist*, and *The Herald Tribune*. During sanctions, however, these items became difficult to come by and were well out of reach of the average Yugoslavian's disposable income. Ironically, sanctions effectively helped give the government a monopoly on news. By restricting the flow of propaganda-free news and opinions, the government-controlled press has little competition and can spout whatever line the regime feels is necessary without fear of contradiction from unbiased sources.

Given this it is no wonder that Serbian moderates such as former Yugoslavian presidential candidate Milan Panic, warned that the embargo that is supposed to bludgeon the extreme nationalists into submission "could have the reverse effect of strengthening the hand of extremists who are trying to persuade Serbs that they are the targets of a global conspiracy."[18] Serbian television and other mass media are for the most part in the hands of nationalists who consistently broadcast messages to "encourage the ostracized Serbs to stand up to what has been cast as a sinister plot to obliterate their nation."[19] Panic warned that "The attempts to punish Serbia are backfiring, rallying support around Serbia's strongman leader Slobodan Milosevic. They think that the sanctions will help get rid of the regime, but it will do otherwise."[20] The more the international community tightens the economic noose around Serbia, Panic and other moderates warn, the less credibility they will have with confused citizens.

These comments indicate that sanctions have been counterproductive for very different reasons from what is advanced here. But even if sanctions did not have this effect of rallying support for Milosevic, they may have been ineffective because of the way they were imposed and enforced. The lax enforcement of the UN resolutions has undercut their effectiveness from the beginning. Smuggling is easy in the Balkans-- there are dozens of obscure border crossings from Romania, Bulgaria, and Albania. There is also river access via the Danube, including past the major oil refining city of Pancevo where tankers made around the clock deliveries during 1992. "After five months of sanctions," claimed one report, "Serbia has secured fresh supplies through a wide network of black marketers."[21] Sanctions have not been rigidly enforced, and their failure may have been mainly due to Yugoslavia's continuing ability to supply itself.

While these are valid points, they cannot fully explain why sanctions appear to have produced an increase in popular support for the Serbian Socialist government of Slobodan Milosevic. First, perhaps sanctions could have been imposed more efficiently, but as the economic reports indicate, sanctions played a role in the continuing economic disintegration of the country, and the nationalist parties responsible for sanctions only became more popular. Secondly, the media is certainly dominated by state-controlled papers and stations, but some opposition media exists and its limited reach seems to be as much a product of limited popular interest as overt suppression. Finally, while the ancient ethnic hatreds thesis appears to have a considerable amount of validity and could certainly be at the root of the conflict, it does not explain the nationalist backlash that accompanied the imposition of sanctions. To fully explain this outcome, we must examine the structural changes sanctions have caused in the Yugoslavian economy, identify the gainers, and determine if they have become politically active.

A STRUCTURAL EXPLANATION OF THE
INEFFECTIVENESS OF SANCTIONS

Serbia's ability to withstand sanctions is partially based on its domestic oil industry. Approximately one-third of its oil is produced domestically, and that is apparently enough to supply the military and essential industries, even if it means severe hardship for ordinary Serbs. Smugglers supply the necessary additional fuel to keep the economy functioning at some minimally acceptable level, albeit at a high cost. In addition to fuel, Serbia is self-sufficient in food production, and its industrial base is able to provide for much of its needs. An indigenous arms industry keeps the military well supplied, and other industries have reaped benefits from sanctions.[22] For example, Feman, a company which producers electrical cables and other electrical equipment, has seen its sales boom in the wake of sanctions and Simpo, a furniture company, experienced significant gains from sanctions.[23] This substitution process builds an elite that is able to extract rents in the form of higher prices for domestically produced import substitutes. Although the model would predict that these manufacturers should be the prime beneficiaries of sanctions and consequently the supporters of the parties and policies that keep sanctions in place, this has not come to pass. Instead, the main gainers from sanctions have been those who control the gasoline smuggling operations.

The one way the international community could successfully impose an unacceptable cost on the Serbian economy was by blocking the export of petroleum products, which are "the chief target of the UN sanctions imposed May 30 1992, with the nations of the Security Council hoping that reduction in supplies of gasoline and heating fuels would encourage Yugoslav citizens to reconsider support for nationalists like Milosevic."[24] As a result of the embargo, by the summer of 1992, "traffic in Serbia all but came to a halt as gas lines became a common sight, snaking through the streets of Belgrade and other cities. Many gas stations closed and tens of thousands were sent on 'forced vacations' because their factories could not run without fuel."[25] If sanctions were truly able to cut off the country from the remaining two-thirds of its supply, the impact on the economy would have been much greater, and sanctions might have had the desired political effect. However, sanctions did not sufficiently deprive Serbia of its fuel supply to provoke a crisis. Instead, half-hearted enforcement opened an opportunity for smugglers to generate huge profits in the illegal gaso-line trade, transferring a tremendous amount of wealth to the Serbian criminal and black market interests. "About 5% to 10% (of the popula-tion) is getting rich off the sanctions," says Dobrivoje Radovanovic, director of the Institute of Criminology in Belgrade. After 18 months of war, "the black market is no longer illegal in Serbia."[26]

Although reliable data is unavailable, we can roughly estimate the profitability of the gasoline trade. Most gasoline was purchased just over the border in Romania and shipped back in private cars specially equipped with door panel and fender tanks or, in places where the Ro-manian border guards are especially lax, in tanker trucks. The price of gasoline(in Deutsche marks) in Romania was stable in 1995-96 at ap-proximately DM .70 per liter, while the price stabilized in Belgrade between DM 2.5 and 3.[27] The gross profit from shipping gasoline from Romania was therefore between DM 1.8 and DM 2.3 per liter, and while no one is certain how much was coming across the border on a daily basis, it would have to at least 100,000 liters per day to keep the price stable.[28] The gross profit from the gasoline trade is approximately DM 200,000 per day, from which bribes, transport costs, and other expenses can be paid, still leaving a phenomenal profit margin.

In addition to those who control the gasoline trade, Dr. Pedrag Simic, director of the Belgrade Institute of International Politics and Economics, claims that it is in the best interests of entire sectors to "have sanctions as long as possible."[29] The remnants of the socialist state-run enterprises, such as steel and heavy industry, enjoy a type of protection as a result of sanctions. They are, in his words, "blessed, they can sell whatever they want and there is no competition," and, as he noted, uncompetitive heavy industry in the rest of the former East Bloc is usually opposed to reforms that expose it to foreign competi-tion. More important, however, the current government benefits from sanctions to an extent. Dr. Dragan Avramovic, the architect of the much-vaunted stabilization program of January 1994, which pegged the Yugoslavian Dinar to the Deutsche mark, admitted in a meeting of economists later that year that Serbia would be "in a deep mess if sanc-tions were lifted tomorrow. Long live sanctions." While this may seem highly counterintuitive, sanctions do provide a level of government revenue that would otherwise be unobtainable because the government charges an "access fee" on goods smuggled into the country, especially gasoline.

The result is that these groups that benefit from sanctions not only have an incentive to keep sanctions in place, but they have the support of the government to some extent. "There is a substantial pro-sanctions lobby," Dr. Simic notes, which he estimates to be at least 10% of the population. In sum, it is simply in the best interests of critical sectors to keep sanctions in place for as long as possible. Not only do sanctions provide a source of protection for industries that would be uncompetitive under free trade conditions, but they are also an important source of revenue for the government. Even more important, sanctions created an immensely profitable black market whose main figures are prominently featured in Serbian politics.

Dr. Jurij Bajec of the Belgrade Economics Institute confirmed this view of the situation but emphasizes the political ramifications of the distortions that sanctions have introduced into the Yugoslavian economy. Although much of the population has suffered as a result of the altered terms of trade and production, "a new class has emerged that got rich quickly in illegal activities." Dr. Bajec went on to add that "They have influenced politics through right wing nationalistic parties. They are using it as a cover for making money."[30] It is not surprising therefore, that the most "right-wing nationalistic parties," the Serbian Radical Party and Arkan's "Group of Citizens," are controlled and funded by the same individuals who control the black market, in some cases with the active help of the Milosevic regime.

The black market functions on two distinct levels. First there are the small-scale entrepreneurs who sell whatever products they were able to slip through the border. This is, for the most part, not a highly profitable sector, and most of those involved would not be doing so except for the fact that upwards of 25% of the population is unemployed and forced to subsist by whatever means it can.[31] The other face of the black market is somewhat more telling for the purposes of this investigation. A small percentage of the population extracts rents from the rest of society through control of the illegal gasoline trade and by forcing consumers to pay a premium price for sanctions-busting imports. The gasoline trade has trickle-down effects through the rest of the economy. Those involved in smuggling have a large disposable income and spend their gains on illegally imported goods, many of which can be bought at a shopping area known as Arkan's Arcade.[32] Arkan is the nom de guerre of paramilitary leader Zeljko Raznjatovic who reportedly controls much of the black market[33] and was an important figure in the 1992 elections. It should not be surprising that his party stood adamantly opposed to any sort of negotiated settlement of the war. Arkan himself is a wealthy man and owes much of his wealth to sanctions, although he has an extended criminal background. It is difficult to verify what percentage of the sanctions-busting traffic Arkan actually controls, but he openly owns the shopping area that features expensive illegally imported goods such as Nike shoes, Benetton clothes, and a wide array of consumer items at premium prices. Even if

Arkan is only acting as landlord and has no hand in the smuggling of the merchandise, he would be making a tidy profit.[34] In 1994, the smallest spaces rented for DM 1500 and larger spaces went for considerably more. There are approximately 50 shops in the arcade which means, assuming the average rent on a store is DM 2000, Arkan is grossing in the neighborhood of 100,000 DM per month from his shopping center.

SERBIAN POLITICS AND POLITICAL PARTIES

It is clear that some proportion of the population has benefited from sanctions despite the general economic downturn Serbia has experienced in recent years. But does this translate into political activity? The political parties of Serbia can be divided into four groups: the ruling Serbian Socialist Party, the ultranationalists, the democratic opposition, and a collection of special interest parties with very limited influence. The Serbian Socialist Party of President Milosevic is the prime instigator of ethnic cleansing and (despite some moves to limit overt support in mid-1994) the supporter of the Bosnian Serbs who are held as primarily responsible for the carnage in Bosnia. How they fared in the elections of 1992 and 1993 is an indicator of how effective sanctions have been in fomenting political change because they instigated the policies that sanctions are aimed at eliminating. The ultranationalists are composed of two parties: Arkan's "Group of Citizens" and the Serbian Radical Party who split away from an earlier coalition with the Socialists to force the 1992 election.[35] The Radicals stand for even stronger prosecution of the war effort. Arkan created his party at Milosevic's behest to draw ultranationalist support away from the Serbian Radical Party. His party was disbanded shortly after the election, but he retained considerable influence. The democratic opposition, known collectively as DEPOS, sought to end the war and sanctions. The difference in the outcomes of the two elections gives some indication as to what effect sanctions had on the political system (see Figure 4.1).

Support for the Serbian Socialist Party increased while support for the democratic opposition and the Serbian Radical Party decreased, a fact that indicates that sanctions have benefited the party responsible for the policies that caused sanctions. While we might expect the Radical Party to have fared better not worse, the government used its control over the media to discredit the leadership of the Serbian Radical Party, which it perceived to be a much greater threat to its continued rule than the democratic opposition.[36] The key point, however, is that the logic of sanctions became inverted. Sanctions are supposed to cause

Figure 4.1
Serbian Elections 1992-1993

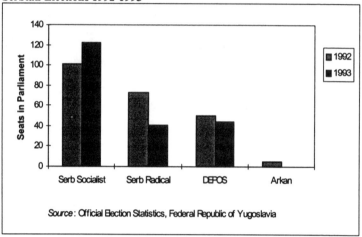

Source: Official Election Statistics, Federal Republic of Yugoslavia

economic pain, which will become translated into political change. But in this case, sanctions appear to have boosted the electoral success of the ruling party.

Sanctions also helped to produce structural changes in the electorate. Of the many political parties in Yugoslavia, the Democratic Party would be one of the best hopes for achieving the goals of the sender countries. The Democratic Party takes a much more moderate stance on the war than the ruling Socialist Party and would aim to comply with the UN resolutions if it came to power. If sanctions had the desired effect, the Democratic Party would become increasingly more popular but in fact, the opposite has happened. According to Dr. Mirolub Labus, Vice-President of the Democratic Party of Serbia, the core constituency of his party was the urban middle class, a group of people that sanctions has helped to eliminate.[37] By driving these people out of the country, the electorate has become more radical and nationalistic. Since this moderate constituency has fled, his party has had to at least make an appearance of moving to the more nationalist right side of the spectrum. " It is a trick," states Dr. Labus, "but it is necessary." Dr. Bajec agrees that this was one of the most noticeable effects of sanctions and that the destruction of the middle class meant that Serbia was "losing the real political force for when changes become necessary. What is generally going to happen under sanctions is counterproductive."

The sanctions could be more effective if they denied profits to the individuals who gained from sanctions and supported the most nationalistic elements in Serbian politics. According to simple supply and demand, we can assume that as sanctions decrease the supply of fuel, profits to smugglers will increase, and for the purposes of the model we can assume that the price increases monotonically at DM .23 per every 100 barrels per day reduction in the supply of fuel. [38] This may or may not be a realistic assumption, but we know the relationship between supply and price is correct. The result is that for every reduction in the supply of fuel, the price goes up and gross profits increase.

The original estimate was that the Serbian economy required 200,000 additional liters (50,000 gallons, 910 barrels) per day of gasoline beyond domestic production to keep the price constant. The price of gasoline is stable at approximately DM 2.5 per liter while the gasoline is purchased in neighboring countries for about DM .7 per liter. The gross profit per gallon is DM 6.8 or

$$(1.8*3.8*50,000= DM\ 342,000).\ [39]$$

If the supply is reduced by 100 Barrels and the price goes up DM .23 the equation changes to:

$$(DM\ 2.73*3.8*45450= 471,498).$$

This would only hold true if demand for oil were completely unaffected by price. This is obviously not the case, but as an essential commodity, oil has a relatively inelastic demand curve. So while demand may fall initially with price increases, at some point the demand curve will flatten out because the economy can only sustain so many reductions in the supply of oil. For the purposes of the model, we can assume that when the supply of oil is cut to 50% of current levels, the demand curve will become flat. Once again, whether or not 50% is an accurate figure is not critical for the purposes of this model. It may be the case that, in reality, the demand curve will flatten before or after this mark, all that is important is that the curve is inelastic at some point.

We can now model the effects of increased oil sanctions against Serbia. Let us assume that the UN was able to reduce the supply of fuel by 100 barrels per day for a month and reduce it a further 100 barrels per day the following month, and so on for each successive month. As Table 4.1 demonstrates, profits to smugglers decrease rather rapidly if oil imports are restricted, suggesting that a strict oil embargo could have been effective. [40] Even when the demand curve flattens out, profits still decrease, albeit less rapidly than before. It is clear that the most nationalistic parties in Serbia are supported by those who have gained financially from sanctions at the expense of the general population. If tightened oil sanctions severely reduce the profitability of the one activity that provides the greatest gains to sanctions profiteers, then we would expect that their motivation to support the nationalist elements responsible for the continuation of ethnic cleansing and other practices that induced sanctions will also be reduced. In short, while sanctions as imposed were in some ways counterproductive, a renewed concentration on oil sanctions could have been highly effective.

Table 4. 1
Model of Oil Sanctions Against Serbia

MONTH	VOLUME (Barl.)	PRICE ($)	DEMAND	GROSS PROFIT (DM 000)
Jan.	910.00	248.00	1.00	225.04
Feb.	819.00	272.80	0.90	200.56
Mar.	737.10	300.08	0.81	178.75
April	663.39	330.09	0.73	159.30
May	597.05	363.10	0.66	141.96
June	537.35	399.41	0.59	126.51
July	483.61	439.35	0.53	112.74
Aug.	435.25	483.28	0.53	111.63
Sept.	391.73	531.61	0.53	110.52
Oct.	352.55	584.77	0.53	109.43
Nov.	317.30	643.25	0.53	108.35
Dec.	285.57	707.57	0.53	107.28
Jan.	257.01	778.33	0.53	106.21

CONCLUSION

This investigation raises the question of when can sanctions be effective, and how they could have been more effective in bringing Serbia into compliance with the United Nations resolutions. There is no question that the Serbian economy is in a shambles, but at the same time, a significant portion of the population has gained financially from the situation. The critical element, therefore, would be to design sanctions so that whatever gains might result from sanctions would be difficult to realize.

Fuel was expected to be the chokepoint by which the international community would compel Serbia to end its expansionist behavior, but instead the illegal gasoline trade has created a class of entrepreneurs who supported the most radical political movements in order to ensure that the source of their profits was not removed. Sanctions could not be effective as long as it was possible to smuggle large amounts of fuel into Serbia.

Most of the fuel crossed into Serbia from either Bulgaria or Romania and could have been controlled. If the United Nations peacekeeping forces, which were been deployed so ineffectively protecting Bosnian "safe havens," had been sent to man checkpoints along the borders that Serbia shares with these two neighbors, the majority of the illegal gasoline trade could be controlled. This is not to say that it would be completely eliminated. Small entrepreneurs could still find ways of avoiding checkpoints and slip a few hundred liters at a time across the border, but this is not what ensured a consistent supply of fuel in the Serbia.

The situation is somewhat similar to Haiti, where gasoline was also supposed to be the chokepoint of the economy. It undoubtedly was, but once again a sector of the population grew rich by transporting gasoline either in coastal ships or across the long and unsecurable border with the Dominican Republic. While in Haiti outside forces would find it nearly impossible to secure such a porous border, the prospects for success of a similar operation in Serbia are much greater. Because of the difference between the two countries' levels of development, Serbia's fuel needs are simply much larger and, unlike Haiti, cannot be sated by small-scale smuggling. An effective blockade of the Romanian and Bulgarian border crossings would reduce Serbia's fuel supplies below the currently sustainable level and provoke a crisis that would have stood a better chance of wringing a compromise from the Milosevic government. At the same time, those who have profited from sanctions would find that they can no longer collect the rents they had become accustomed to and would have little reason to support the extreme nationalist elements whose actions ensure the continuation of sanctions.

There are several clear lessons to be learned from this case. First, sanctions that disrupt trade will create groups of gainers with an incentive to lobby for the continuance of the policies that prompted sanctions. However, there will always be chokepoints in an economy that can be exploited. Petroleum is, of course, the most obvious and, although the use of petroleum sanctions has often failed, they could nonetheless be a highly effective means of forcing target countries to comply with the demands of the senders. Such a strategy failed to compel Rhodesia to renounce the Unilateral Declaration of Independence (UDI), but this was mainly because Rhodesia was able to satisfy its minimum fuel needs with the cooperation of South Africa. Had there been stringent enforcement of the sanctions aimed at cutting off the flow of South African transshipments, the Rhodesian government could not have maintained the degree of popularity it did among white Rhodesians for very long. Rigorously enforced sanctions aimed at products with highly inelastic demand curves that the target country cannot produce domestically can be effective. Had more attention been given to this point when sanctions were initially imposed against Serbia, they could have played a role in controlling this latest spasm of violence in the Balkans.

The second lesson to be learned from this case is that carefully targeted financial sanctions could have been more effective. Had trade been allowed to continue freely, but credits, loan guarantees, and aid of any kind been suspended, the Yugoslavian government would be in a serious predicament, and there would be no constituency interested in seeing that this sort of sanction stayed in place. But export sanctions formed a constituency that not only wants to see them maintained, but also has the resources to fund political campaigns of nationalist parties whose actions keep sanctions in place. Had only financial sanctions been implemented, such a group would simply not exist. In addition, the government's fiscal problems would possibly be even more acute because it would not have the benefit of revenue from the gasoline trade that it collects in the form of access fees.

This case is important not just because it offers a testing ground for the theory of sanctions but also because it is a critical test of the international community's ability to control regional instability. Economic sanctions were a critical part of the international effort to end the war in Bosnia, but we must view them as part of a much grander scheme. As the Cold War recedes further and further into history, Balkan-style conflicts will probably become more prominent, and how sanctions can and cannot be used to control them will become increasingly relevant.

NOTES

1. Laura Silber and Alan Little, *Yugoslavia: Death of a Nation* (London: TV Books, 1996), 277.

2. Economist Intelligence Unit, *Country Profile: Yugoslavia (Serbia-Montenegro), Macedonia 1996-97* (1997), 19.

3. Federal Statistical Office, *Basic Data on Socio-Economic Movements* (Belgrade, Yugoslavia: Presse-Express, 1993), 2.

4. "Serbs Have Faith in their New Saviour," *The Financial Times*, 9 May 1994, 4.

5. Inflation was brought under control with the introduction of the New Dinar in January 1994, which tied the currency to the German Deutsche mark. Before this radical step was taken, inflation ran at nearly 20% per day. While the currency is now fairly stable, prices on all but the most basic goods are out of range for most wage-earners. Salaries average around 200 Dinar per month, but the cost of living (excluding housing) is only marginally lower than in Western Europe, and some items, such as gasoline, are made prohibitively

expensive by sanctions.

6. One is constantly amazed by the bitterness the different groups express toward one another. One university-educated Serb told me that the Muslims and ethnic Albanians had less respect for life because "they have twenty children at a time, what do they care if one or two get killed in battles with Serbs?"

7. "The Bitter Balkan War Offers Tragic Parallels to the Mideast Stalemate," *Wall Street Journal,* 7 October 1992, A1.

8. Franjo Tudjman, *Nationalism in Contemporary Europe* (Boulder: East European Monographs, 1981), 151.

9. Ibid., p.154.

10. Lenard Cohen, "Balkan Consociationalism: Ethnic Representation and Ethnic Distance in Yugoslav Elites" in *War and Society in East Central Europe Volume X, At the Brink of War and Peace: The Tito-Stalin Split in Historical Perspective,* ed. Wayne S. Vucinich (New York: Brooklyn College Press Social Science Monographs, 1982, 35.

11. In what seemed to be a deliberately provocative move, Croatia changed the name of its currency in 1994 to the Kuna, a symbol culled from the fascist era.

12. Ministry of Information of the Republic of Serbia, *A Dictionary of Misconceptions: A Hundred Falsities About Serbia and How to Answer Them* (Belgrade, Yugoslavia: Ministry of Information, 1994), 185.

13. Telephone interview with Vladimir Matic, May 18, 1994.

14. Marko Milivojevic, *Descent Into Chaos: Yugoslavia's Worsening Crisis,* European Security Study No. 7 (London: Institute for European Defence and Strategic Studies 1989), 8.

15. Ibid.

16. Ivo Bicanic, "Fractured Economy," in *Yugoslavia: A Fractured Federalism,* ed. Dennison Rusinow (Washington, DC: Wilson Center Press, 1988).

17. "Serbia Leader Draws on Reserve of Anger at Outside World in Elections," *Los Angeles Times ,* 20 December 1993, A4.

18. "Tougher Yugoslav Sanctions Unlikely to Get Fast Results," *Los Angeles Times,* 19 November 1992. A1.

19. Ibid.

20. Ibid.

21. Ibid.

22. The Zastava Arms Factory has introduced new products since sanctions, including the CZ-99 handgun.

23. Interview with Mihaljo Rabrenovic, Chief of Staff, Serbian Ministry of the Economy, August 15, 1994.

24. "Tougher Yugoslav Sanctions Unlikely to Get Fast Results."

25. "U. N. Authorizes Naval Blockade Against Serbia," *Los Angeles Times,* 18 November 1992, A22.

26. Ibid.

27. Interview with Harvey Lee, Economic Officer, United States Embassy, Belgrade Yugoslavia. August 9, 1994.

28. Ibid. The figure may be as high as 200,000 liters.

29. Interview with Dr. Predrag Simic, Director, Institute of International

Politics and Economics, Belgrade, Yugoslavia, August 10, 1994.

30. Interview with Dr. Jurij Bajec, Director, Belgrade Economics Institute, Belgrade, Yugoslavia, August 12, 1994.

31. There are some very profitable niches. Some individuals I met specialized in high value-added items, such as computer parts and cosmetics, and they appeared to be doing quite well by Yugoslavian standards.

32. Before sanctions, luxury cars, such as Mercedes and BMWs, were a rare sight in the streets of Belgrade. After several years of sanctions, they are commonplace, especially outside of the cafes and restaurants favored by smugglers.

33. "Serb Warlord's Truly Shotgun Wedding," *Los Angeles Times*, 20 February 1995. A8.

34. The shopping center is also an excellent money-laundering operation.

35. Arkan's party was less a political movement than a means of gaining political control over the Kosovo smuggling operation. His main interest in Kosovo was "grabbing a slice of the black market which the local Albanian mafias were forced to share with him." Tim Judah, *The Serbs: History, Myth and the Destruction of Yugoslavia* (New Haven: Yale University Press, 1997), 186.

36. Milosevic helped Seselj and the Serbian Radical Party get elected by giving them large blocks of time on government controlled TV. Seselj supported Milosevic, but this began to fall apart when he thought he was powerful enough to challenge Milosevic for the Presidency. In 1993, Milosevic turned on Seselj and made him a scapegoat for all the accusations being leveled against the Serbs in the war. An SPS statement issued in September calls Seselj "the personification of violence and criminality" and accuses him of war profiteering. (Judah, p. 255).

37. Interview with Dr. Mirolub Labus, Vice-President of the Democratic Party of Serbia, Belgrade, Yugoslavia, August 16, 1994.

38. 100 barrels is an arbitrary figure. The model could just as easily function with a smaller or larger figure.

39. The 3.8 multiplier is used to convert liters to gallons. There are 55 gallons in a barrel.

40. Gross profit is calculated by [(volume*price)*demand]. Demand decreases by 10% with each increase in price until supply is at 50% of current.

5

Sanctions Against Iraq

How has Saddam Hussein been able to survive, and in some ways prosper, under sanctions?[1] Many observers in 1990 believed that economic sanctions against Iraq could succeed if they were imposed quickly and if sufficient international cooperation was achieved in blocking Iraq's access to imported goods, especially anything that could enable it to continue its aggressive behavior against neighboring states.[2] Although sanctions had a devastating effect on the Iraqi economy, they did not have the desired political effect either before or after the Gulf War, presenting a paradox that eludes conventional explanation.

The debate over the use of sanctions as opposed to military force that took place in late 1990 was divided between those who argued that sanctions would be an effective means of forcing the Iraqi army from Kuwait and those who claimed that sanctions would fail through a lack of international cooperation in their enforcement. While both of these schools of thought have their merits, they are both fundamentally flawed because they fail to take into account the structural changes that trade disrupting sanctions tend to induce over time. This case demonstrates the differing effects of import and export sanctions. Iraq's economy was severely damaged by the international effort to block oil exports, its main source of export earnings. While stringent import sanctions denied Iraq most of its export earnings, export sanctions prompted import substitution and increased government control over the economy.

The idea that sanctions would have been effective if they had been left in place longer ignores the lessons of the past. The sanctions used against Iraq included a blockade of most exports, with the exception of those items that could be designated as humanitarian shipments.[3] This action was supposed to reduce Iraq's ability to wage war, but given its level of development and experience with producing spare parts substitutes for imported weapons developed during the Iran-Iraq war, it should have been obvious that this blockade would prompt import substitution. While industry is still fairly limited in Iraq, it has some capacity to produce sophisticated military equipment, including ballistic missiles, and chemical, biological, and (without the intercession of the Israeli Air Force in 1981) nuclear weapons.

One element of the UN mandated sanctions should have had increasingly devastating effects over time: the ban on Iraqi oil sales. These import sanctions attacked the source of the overwhelming majority of Iraq's export earnings. If sanctions could truly prevent Iraq from selling its oil on the world market, its foreign reserves would be rapidly depleted, prompting a economic crisis that could in fact bring about Iraqi compliance with the UN resolutions. Compounded with the fact that the Iraqi economy was already severely weakened after eight years of relentless war with Iran, many experts predicted success for the embargo. "Tracking and enforcing an embargo against Iraqi-controlled oil exports should not be a big problem," said Henry Schuller of the Center for International and Strategic Affairs. "The problem will be sustaining the commitment."[4]

To some extent, those who argued that sanctions were ineffective because of insufficient international cooperation in their enforcement were correct. A decreasing level of international cooperation allowed Iraq to slip enough oil through to mitigate the effects of this form of economic warfare. Iraq has been reportedly selling upwards of 100,000 barrels of oil a day throughout the embargo.[5] By making side payments to Kurdish leaders (who were only recently fighting the Hussein regime), convoys of tanker trucks are allowed to carry oil through Kurdish territory in Northern Iraq to destinations in Iran and Turkey where it is resold. Small tankers also make their way from the port of Umm Qasr near Basra to ports in the Persian Gulf near Dubai, where the oil is transferred to larger tankers destined for the Mediterranean.[6]

Iraqi oil is extremely cheap, and many traders are willing to take the risk that they will be caught by the (mostly American) forces enforcing sanctions. Even so, until 1998, when the UN raised the limit on Iraqi oil sales to nearly pre-war levels, Iraq was only able to generate a fraction of the nearly $13 billion per year it was earning before the war. Although the oil smuggling operations are directed by the government, many privately owned companies are also involved in the illegal oil trade. The central purpose of the whole operation is to obtain hard currency to keep the country's food rationing system functioning. Since the rationing system is one of the prime means of maintaining a minimally acceptable standard of living for the Iraqi population, the illegal oil trade is critical to keeping the Hussein regime in power, as well as maintaining the ruling clan's luxurious lifestyle.

European oil companies are eager to exploit the underutilized Iraqi reserves and have reportedly concluded talks with the Hussein regime to drill and export Iraqi oil once sanctions are lifted, and they plan to boost oil production to 5 million barrels per day, double what it was producing before sanctions.[7] These openings have been encouraged by the French and Russian governments, which have taken the position that sanctions have gone on long enough.[8] This attitude is partially born of the fact that Iraq's oil reserves are second only to Saudi Arabia's, and because the French government feels it has been slighted by the resolution of the Gulf War. The French contend that the United States has excluded its European allies from the lucrative defense and rebuilding contracts resulting from the war, and they have used this as a justification for contradicting the United States and opposing the continuation of sanctions in the UN Security Council. These actions indicate that, as predicted by sanctions critics, the international cooperation that makes the oil sales embargo effective breaks down over time. At the same time, those who focus solely on the level of international cooperation ignore the ability of target countries such as Iraq to adjust to the trade distorting effects of export sanctions and the political ramifications this distortion may have.

Many respected foreign policy professionals and commentators went on record in favor of economic sanctions against Iraq. In testimony before the Senate Armed Services Committee, former chief of the Joint Chiefs of Staff Admiral William J. Crowe Jr. argued that "We should give sanctions a fair chance before we discard them. I personally believe that they will bring him (Saddam Hussein) to his knees ultimately. If the sanctions work in 12-18 months instead of six months, the trade-off of avoiding war with its attendant sacrifices and uncertainties would, in my estimation, be more than worth it."[9] Henry Kissinger was more guarded in his comments, but did suggest that they could be successful in bringing about a negotiated settlement. "If sanctions bite within a time frame relevant to political processes," he stated before the Senate Armed Services Committee, "Iraq is more likely to negotiate."[10] Marine Corps commandant General Alfred M. Gray told a group of retired Marines and defense contractors, "I keep saying 'What's the hurry here? Time is on our side, not Saddam's.'" [11]

Even President George Bush was optimistic early on about the potential for sanctions to compel Iraq into compliance with the United Nations resolutions. "Economic sanctions in this instance if fully enforced can be very, very effective," said the president in a speech on August 8, 1990. "There are some indications that he's (Hussein) already beginning to feel the pinch and nobody can stand up forever to total economic deprivation."[12] Crowe, Gray, Kissinger, and Bush are by no measure the most dovish voices in Washington, yet all of them at some point in the debate believed that economic sanctions could force Iraq from Kuwait.

The trade statistics on Iraq suggest that it would be particularly vulnerable to economic pressure. Thirty percent of its prewar GNP went to pay for imports, much of it food, and most of its export earnings came from oil. Oil sales accounted for nearly 95% of its export earnings, and oil production was equal to almost 40% of GDP.[13] Iraq is also highly dependent on foreign trade, which forms a significant percentage of GDP: 35%-50% for both exports and imports as compared to the 25% average for middle-income countries.[14] Its industry was based primarily on the assembly of foreign-produced goods, further intensifying its reliance on imports. Finally, Iraq is a relatively easy country to blockade. Its oil is shipped through pipelines to Turkey, which could be shut with the turn of a valve or via trucks through Jordan or from its ports on the gulf coast, all of which could be easily blockaded. All things considered, Iraq seemed to be an ideal candidate for economic sanctions.

Whatever the effect of sanctions on the Iraqi economy, many critics argued that the economic devastation of the country would have very little effect on Saddam Hussein's calculations and decisions. Saddam Hussein rules through fear and intimidation, often using the secret police to snuff out any opposition inside or outside the regime. One psychologist who testified before the Senate hearings stated that Saddam Hussein is "surrounded by sycophants who are cowed by Saddam's well-founded reputation for brutality and are afraid to contradict him."[15] Even if this economic pressure directed against the Iraqi people succeeded in driving living standards below tolerable levels, there was little chance that Saddam would not be able to control popular unrest. Within the elite circle surrounding him, he is completely intolerant of any criticism as exemplified by an infamous 1984 cabinet meeting in which the Iraqi leader invited criticism only to have the one minister who accepted the invitation brutally killed as a lesson to those who would dare to be anything less than completely subservient. It was clear that economic pressure directed against the Iraqi people would not necessarily translate into pressure against Saddam given the level of personal control he exerts over the population. These factors led Director of Central Intelligence William Webster to conclude that "There is no assurance or guarantee that the economic hardships will compel Saddam to change his policies or lead to internal unrest that would threaten his regime."[16]

This testimony did not deter sanctions proponents who countered that even if sanctions could not directly force Saddam to back down, they would at least weaken Iraq's ability to fight. "Why not give sanctions time to work?" asked Arthur Schlesinger in early 1991. "The Central Intelligence Agency already reports shortages in Iraq's military spare parts. If we must fight, why not fight a weaker rather than a stronger Iraq? What is the big rush?"[17] While Iraq is a relatively advanced country by third world standards, Schlesinger held that it simply cannot even begin to produce spare parts for sophisticated military equipment.

But Iraq did produce spare parts and found ways of extending the life of existing equipment. The effectiveness of sanctions against the Iraqi military may have been only temporary, and giving sanctions more time to work, as many in Congress and elsewhere argued, may not have been the best course of action. This is not to say that sanctions failed to have a disastrous effect on the Iraqi economy. Quite to the contrary, it appears that sanctions were highly effective in wreaking havoc on the economy, but it is precisely because they were effective economically but not politically that makes it an interesting case to investigate. This case also provides an excellent example of the difference between the effects of import and export sanctions. The oil blockade appears to have been highly damaging to Iraq, but the export sanctions appear to have prompted import substitution, especially in the agricultural sector. In addition, sanctions have placed more of Iraqi economy under state control, giving Saddam Hussein even tighter direct control of the country.

USING FOOD AS A WEAPON: AGRICULTURAL SANCTIONS AGAINST IRAQ

Information on the Iraqi economy was scarce even before sanctions, which makes it difficult to ascertain the country's adjustment and import substitution capacity. However, there is some information on Iraqi agriculture, which can serve as a proxy by which we can gauge the substitution process in other sectors of the economy. Iraq was a major importer of food and nowhere near being self-sufficient, even in staple crops such as wheat and rice, before the Gulf War. Accordingly, U. S. intelligence estimates at the beginning of the conflict in August

1990 estimated that Iraq would run low in food within a few months.[18] A hungry population is an unruly one, and the Hussein regime would soon have to give into the demands of the international community if it was to be able to meet the population's most basic needs.

Iraqi agricultural production was an important indicator of how the country responded to sanctions. Iraq was clearly capable of producing more food that it did before sanctions. While 50% of the country is arable, only 11% of the land was used for agriculture before the war. While dwarfed by oil, agriculture was an important sector of the economy in terms of employment. Nearly 30% of the labor force was involved in agriculture. Iraq depended heavily on food imports, because it was economically to its advantage to sell oil and buy food. Once trade was cut off, the Hussein regime scrambled to make the country more self-sufficient in food and achieved considerable success. Agriculture began to play a much larger role in the Iraqi economy beginning with 1990.

It is difficult to separate the effects of the war from the effects of sanctions after 1991. But in 1990, we can observe the effects of sanctions without interference from the effects of the bombing campaign and insurrections which followed. In 1989-90 the wheat harvest amounted to 1.2 million metric tons. In 1990-91, however, the harvest was nearly 1.5 million metric tons, or a 24% increase.[19] Fifty percent more land was planted with cereals in the second period.[20]

Iraqi agriculture was in disarray long before the imposition of sanctions. As one analyst noted, "The ready availability of cheap food imports (nearly half from the United States) along with two decades of collectivized agriculture under the socialist Baathist party has left Iraq dependent on imports for three-quarters of its food."[21] But sanctions prompted a significant recovery in the agricultural sector. The 1990 harvest included 1.2 metric tons of wheat and 1.9 metric tons of barley, which compares favorably to the largest harvest on record (1985 with 1.4 million tons of wheat and 1.3 million tons of barley[22]).

Iraqi agriculture experienced a boom of unprecedented proportions after the imposition of sanctions. This was closely orchestrated by the government, as it took pains to ensure that the incentives to produce introduced by sanctions were magnified through a series of decrees and programs. The steps taken by the Revolutionary Command Council (RCC) can be divided into three categories: First, decrees that imposed severe penalties on those farmers or landowners who failed to use their land to its fullest capacity: Second, programs that made it cheaper and ultimately more profitable to produce agricultural products: and third, programs designed to expand the amount of arable land.

The RCC realized that if it was to achieve anything approaching agricultural self-sufficiency, it would have to see, first and foremost, that currently available farmland was used to its fullest extent. Only days after sanctions were imposed, the RCC issued Decree No. 367 which stated "All lands not planted by their owners or others in accordance with the scheduled agricultural density shall be considered state property without remuneration."[23]   Later the government announced that arable land leased from the state that was not "properly used" would be confiscated and lent to others who would fulfill the government's agricultural development goals.[24] The message to Iraqi landowners was clear: Use it or lose it, and most cooperated with the government.

But the RCC's approach was not all stick and no carrot. In an effort to keep the cost of farm labor down, agricultural workers were exempted from military service.[25] The government also made it easier for farmers to obtain credit. The Ministry of Agriculture announced on September 30, 1990, that it would increase loans to farmers by 100%, pay for some seeds and fertilizers, and offer additional loans totaling 586 million Dinars.[26]   That same month, the Ministry of Agriculture increased the purchasing price for corn, wheat, and barley, providing an additional incentive for farmers to produce basic grains.[27]   In an added effort to sweeten the pot, Baghdad radio reported in November that farmers could cultivate state-owned land with cereals at no cost, which soon put more than 230,000 plots of government-owned land in the hands of farmers.[28] The RCC believed that by offering incentives to produce above and beyond what market forces were already doing, and by penalizing those who did not take the additional risks of added production, they would be able to dramatically increase food production in Iraq. By most accounts it appears that they were basically correct.

In October 1990, the RCC set out to draw up a comprehensive agricultural plan "utilizing and exploiting every inch of Iraqi arable lands."[29]   Although Iraqi reports undoubtedly exaggerated whatever gains were made, there was a significant expansion in arable land. The Governor of the province of Al-Barah noted that there had been a huge increase in the amount of land under cultivation in his region. In 1980, the amount of land under cultivation was 16,445 donums, which increased to 45,046 in 1990 (a donum equals 2,500 square meters).[30] Although this growth is not completely due to sanctions, a good portion of the increase is the result of the RCC's quest for self-sufficiency.

The results of this expansion are seen in the production statistics. The Baghdad newspaper *Al-Jumhimiya* reported in September 1990 that dairy production increased 26% over the previous year, and vegetable production increased 2.5 times over the previous year's harvest from 1 million tons in 1989 to 2.5 million tons in 1990.[31] In November 1990, the Iraqi government began a land reclamation program to increase output, which they claim yielded an additional 190,000 donums of arable land and was projected to bring a further 200,000 donums into production within a year.[32] In addition, major renovations of existing irrigation canals and construction of new ones began in order to bring water to the new areas.

While official Iraqi statistics should be taken with a large grain of salt, and there have been reports of inadequate food supplies, the agricultural production program met with some success. Shortly after the war ended, agricultural production had increased enough to allow increases in monthly flour rations from 7 kilograms to 8.[33] In addition, some western reporters noticed ample food supplies before and after the war, describing markets where "shelves sag beneath the weight of fresh fruit, vegetables, and fish."[34]

This agricultural expansion had some spin-offs in the manufacturing sector. Sixteen rural workshops were built for the farm machinery maintenance and parts manufacture,[35] and Iraq experimented with new methods of tire re-treading to extend the life of farm equipment.[36] In addition, new irrigation projects were started and new wells were dug in an effort to fulfill Iraq's expanded need for water. While this is not very dramatic, sanctions did unleash some amount of indigenous ingenuity in a number of ways, which contributed to the country's ability to withstand sanctions.

The food embargo was expected to reduce the Iraqi standard of living to the point that Saddam Hussein would be forced to back down in his standoff with the UN, but Iraq was apparently able to adapt remarkably well. Sanctions should theoretically have the greatest potential to influence a country's behavior when the embargoed products have a particularly inelastic demand curve. In the case of Iraq, it was expected that food would be an effective weapon because of its inelasticity: No society can function for long without a source of basic foodstuffs. But Iraq did not produce much of its food because it could import more efficiently. Before sanctions, Iraq bought approximately 3.8 million tons of wheat annually, mostly from the United States and Australia, as well as rice and sugar. Once imports were screened out, Iraq found its potential to produce much of what it needed. Considering that sanctions were supposed to play off Iraq's reliance on imported food, the fact that it has now achieved some measure of self-sufficiency only demonstrates the perverse effects that sanctions can and do have. Iraq is now more agriculturally self-sufficient than before sanctions, which leaves it significantly less vulnerable to international pressure of this type in the future.

There is no doubt that the Iraqi people are suffering from a lack of basic foodstuffs. The Food and Agricultural Organization (FAO) has found in numerous reports that only the basic rationing program keeps the population from starvation. But we must be aware that it was the devastation from the war and the subsequent civil strife that destroyed the ability of Iraq to bolster its food production program. As the experience of 1990 indicates, Iraq was well on its way to becoming less dependent on food imports.

Although Iraq has been severely damaged by sanctions, the 30% of the population involved in agriculture has benefited. Prices for basic commodities rose precipitously. By June 1993, the price of wheat on the open market had increased 355 times. The political effect of this substitution process was to build a constituency that had a distinct interest in seeing that sanctions stayed in place. Although it is difficult to calculate exactly because of the lack of data, there is no doubt that Iraqi farmers benefited tremendously from sanctions. In addition to the variety of government subsidies and programs that sprang up in the wake of sanctions, they were given a captive market, and Hussein has been able to use this to his political benefit.

Two-thirds of Iraq's crops are grown in the central region of the country, which coincidentally is the region where Hussein has the strongest support. The ruling Tikriti group has its tribal base of support in the central regions of al-Dhulaym and Jubr. Virtually the entire ruling elite of Iraq has its familial roots in this region.[37] This is precisely the region that benefits most from the increased reliance on domestic foodstuffs brought about by sanctions. By supporting agriculture, Hussein has been able to twist the impact of sanctions such that they reward his support base in the central Iraqi countryside.

THE IMPACT OF SANCTIONS ON IRAQI INDUSTRY

In 1992, *The Economist* noted that, despite the embargo, much of the Iraqi economy was managing to function. "Given the grim circumstances and in the absence of spare parts and supplies, the Iraqi economy has coped surprisingly well."[38] It is difficult to accurately gauge the impact of sanctions on Iraqi industry because of the lack of data. The Iraqi government stopped publishing data on industrial production during the Gulf War; however, there is a substantial amount of evidence available from the Federal Broadcast Information Service (FBIS) transcripts of Iraqi media, and from it we can piece together a more complete picture of how sanctions have affected the Iraqi economy.

Saddam Hussein himself claimed that sanctions have been counterproductive, boasting that the international economic boycott had helped Iraq to become more self-sufficient. "The embargo has provided us with an opportunity to organize the economy, define emergency plans and harness available resources without relying solely on the wealth of oil," the Iraqi leader was quoted as saying by Baghdad newspapers.[39]

It is difficult to parse out the effects of sanctions because of the confounding effect of the war and the fact that Iraq was engaging in ISI long before sanctions were imposed. The Iraqi economy has featured heavy state involvement since the ruling Baath Party took power in 1968. Baathist ideology is a quasi-socialist, nationalist set of ideas that funded large state-owned enterprises in the name of furthering the Iraqi people and the Arab nation as a whole, so in some ways sanctions served as a means to advance the industrial development goals of the regime. Qadisiya State Enterprise for Electric Industries, for example, has claimed success in its ISI drive. Between July 1989 and March 1990, it saved $21 million by using local suppliers and planned to cut total imports over five years from $231 million to $16 million.[40]

Iraq has been fairly successful in producing substitutes for some manufactured items. After the Gulf War, the Military Industrialization Organization (MIO) under the leadership of General Hussein Kamel Hassan (who defected to Jordan in August 1995) was charged with developing import substitutes. By April 1992, the MIO had designed and built a completely indigenous tractor, with 2,000 scheduled for the first production run.[41] This was an interesting development in and of itself, but it cannot be ignored that many of the same parts and mechanical skills that are necessary for a heavy-duty tractor can be used for building military vehicles such as armored personnel carriers and mounts for mobile guns, as well as spare parts for leftover Soviet weaponry. In addition, the Ministry of Industry and Military Industrialization (MIMI) announced local production of General Motors cars. Local components for Oldsmobile, Buick, and Pontiac are being manufactured, and Iraq has the capability to produce 50% of the models that were under production before sanctions.

Of course ISI is usually regarded as an inefficient means of development, channeling resources into show projects and producing goods of substandard quality, and in the case of Iraq, there is no doubt that these problems have plagued Iraq's quest for industrial self-sufficiency. The Iraqi Central Organization for Standardization and Quality Control released a report in May 1990 claiming that 22% of state sector industrial products were defective or substandard.[42] But if ISI is economically unproductive when alternatives are available, its attractiveness increases when imports are constrained by external forces such as sanctions. We also must consider the political benefits of this developmental strategy. ISI allows the state to become the main allocator of economic benefits, thereby creating a constituency that should be aware that its interests are firmly tied to the survival of the regime. In this case, the primary spur to this ISI drive is externally imposed. Just as benefactors from ISI in other countries tend to lobby for the maintenance of tariffs long after the protection is no longer warranted, the benefactors from sanctions should rationally take measures to encourage the government of Iraq to maintain the policies that keep sanctions in place. By concentrating the power to allocate resources in the hands of the state, it gives the Iraqi leadership the ability to reward its supporters and punish the less enthusiastic members of the business community.

One example of this is readily apparent in Iraq's agricultural strategy. The Iraqi government issued a number of decrees designed to weaken the hand of urban merchants who also stood to gain from sanctions but were denied any profits through government decrees. In November 1990, the RCC set down rules to "firmly punish those hoarders who fail to market crops and levy penalties equal to those related to sabotaging the economy." At the same time the government declared itself the sole legitimate grain dealer, effectively wiping out an entire sector of urban merchants. The regime also strove to eliminate the hoarding of food in the countryside by declaring that any attempts to hold back crops from the new state-run agricultural buying board would be punishable by death.[43]

There were several stages to the Iraqi government's reaction to sanctions, and at each stage the regime was able to increase its control over the economy and direct the brunt of the effects against its enemies. In the first stage the government gained control over the agricultural sector of the economy. We have already seen how Hussein was able to dramatically increase agricultural production by increasing the incentives to produce and punishing those who did not wholeheartedly support the government's plans, but these actions had another effect: They served to centralize control of the rural economy in the hands of the government. The regime instituted controls over marketing of farm products in 1991. By October 1992, the government was buying up grain harvests well below free market price in an attempt to maintain the support of the consuming public.[44]

In addition, price controls were reinstituted after they had been removed in August 1990. In the summer of 1992, the government announced that it would no longer tolerate overcharging and hoarding, executing 40 merchants to make its point. As Patrick Clawson notes, this had a tendency to force the trade in many goods underground. "Merchants have been understandably reluctant to repeat their efforts to supply Iraq's needs, for fear of incurring new government penalties instead of rewards."[45] The effect was to give the government even tighter control over the economy and reduce the autonomy of the middle-class traders and merchants who might be prone to support opposition groups.

In the next stage, the regime tightened its control over the monetary system. In May 1993, the old 25 Dinar notes were declared no longer valid and could only be exchanged within Iraq. The reason given was to counteract counterfeiting, but in fact the old notes were more highly valued because they were of higher quality in terms of printing and paper stock, and exchanged for three times that of the new ones on the black market. The real reason behind the move was to hurt holders of the old notes: Kurds in the north who held 1.3 billion of the old notes and could not exchange them with the autonomous Kurdish government and Iraqi merchants in Jordan who held some 3 billion Dinars of the now worthless notes.

Each of these moves was instituted ostensibly to counteract the effects of sanctions, but they served another purpose: to increase government control over the economy. The government was able to use that increased control to punish enemies and potential sources of opposition to the regime. The price controls severely hurt the merchant class in Iraq while the monetary policy served to economically devastate enemies, both potential and active, outside of Iraq proper. Sanctions were supposed to weaken Saddam Hussein's grip on Iraqi society, but in a perverse manner sanctions forced him to recentralize control over the economy in a way that served to tighten his hold on Iraq.

Sanctions have had mixed effects on Iraq. Although the oil blockade has been successful in denying the country its main source of foreign exchange, export sanctions appear to have prompted some import substitution. It must be noted that this study has, for a lack of other sources, relied heavily on the Iraqi media, which is far from reliable. But the Iraqi media has gone to great lengths to depict the suffering sanctions have caused in an attempt to garner international sympathy, so it does not seem to be in their best interests to trumpet examples of Iraq's ability to cope with sanctions.

This study raises the obvious question of how sanctions could have been more effective. The insulation of the Hussein regime from the general population combined with Hussein's remarkable ability to avoid coups and assassination attempts means that the link between economic depravation, popular discontent, and policy change is extremely weak in this case.

Sanctions alone will not remove Saddam Hussein from power, but the blockade of Iraqi oil sales was an effective means of denying the regime its main source of hard currency. If combined with other tools to support indigenous rebels and stringent export controls on items that could be used for rearmament, the oil blockade could be a important part of ending the ongoing stalemate that has brought misery to most Iraqis and little benefit to American national security interests. Yet over time, the international cooperation which kept the blockade intact has withered and there is no sign that the original goal of post-war sanctions, elimination of Iraq's nuclear, chemical, and biological weapons, is close to being achieved. Economic sanctions have failed, but not because they failed to impose a significant cost on Iraq. They have failed because the most effective part of the sanctions package, the oil embargo, was leaky enough to support the regime, and because the sanctions were not combined with other measures in a strategic manner. The historical lessons are clear enough: Sanctions are rarely enough on their own to drive a regime from power, but in the case of Iraq there was an opportunity to combine effective sanctions with other tools to end the reign of Saddam Hussein.

NOTES

1. Patrick Clawson, *How Has Saddam Hussein Survived? Economic Sanctions, 1990-1993*, Institute for National Strategic Studies, National Defense University McNair Paper 22, September 1993.

2. Kimberly Ann Elliott, "Sanctions Will Bite and Soon," *New York Times*, 3 August 1990, A27.

3. U. N. Security Council Resolution 660 of August 6, 1990 states, "all states shall prevent the sale or supply by their nationals or from their territories or using their flag vessels of any commodities or products, including weapons or any other military equipment, whether or not originating in their territories, but not including supplies intended strictly for medical purposes, and, in humanitarian circumstances, foodstuffs to any person or body in Iraq or Kuwait."

4. "Experts Say Embargo May Work if Nations Maintain Commitment," *New York Times*, 6 August 1990, A1.

5. "The Dhows that do the Iraqi Run," *The Economist*, 25 April 1998, p. 27.

6. "Iraq Said to Sell Oil in Secret Plan to Skirt U. N. Ban," *New York Times*, 16 February 1995, A1.

7. Given the trend of oil prices in the 1990s, this seems to be overstated. At current prices, it would be difficult to justify the capital investment required to double production. Iraq's oil reserves are higher than many other oil producing countries because its state-owned drilling facilities are fairly primitive by current standards.

8. "Iraq, Russia Agree on Oil Projects for Embargo's End," *The Wall Street Journal*, 12 February 1995, A5.

9. William J. Crowe Jr., Admiral (ret.), Testimony before the United States Senate Armed Services Committee, November 28, 1990.

10. Henry Kissinger, Testimony before the United States Senate Armed Services Committee, November 28, 1990.

11. Les Aspin, The Aspin Papers: Sanctions, Diplomacy and War in the Persian Gulf (Washington, D.C.: The Center for International and Strategic Studies, 1991), 17.

12. George Bush, Speech of August 8, 1990. Cited in M. Cifry and C. Cerf, eds., *The Gulf War Reader* (New York: Random House, 1991), 199.

13. Clawson, p.12.

14. Ibid.

15. Ibid., 20.

16. Ibid., 19.

17. Arthur Schlesinger Jr., "White Slave in the Persian Gulf," *The Wall Street Journal*, 7 January 1991.

18. Economist Intelligence Unit, *Quarterly Economic Report on Iraq*, 4 (1990): 11.

19. United Nations Food and Agricultural Organization, *Special Alert 237, FAO WFP Crop and Food Supply Assessment Mission to Iraq*, July 1993, p.8

20. United Nations Food and Agricultural Organization, *Global Information and Early Warning System on Food and Agriculture Special Alert 223*, July 22, 1991, p. 3.

21. *National Review,* 31 December 1990, 42: no. 25. p. 12.

22. Ibid.

23. Federal Broadcast Information Service Middle Eastern Daily Report (FBIS), 11 September 1990, p. 41.

24. FBIS, 4 October 1990, p. 27.

25. FBIS, 11 September 1990, p. 42.

26. FBIS, 3 October 1990, p. 25.

27. FBIS, 5 October 1990, p. 27.

28. FBIS, 9 November 1990, p. 28.

29. FBIS, 26 September 1990, p. 36.

30. FBIS, 18 September 1990, p. 37.

31. FBIS, 18 October 1990, p. 28.

32. FBIS, 9 November 1990, p. 28.

33. FBIS, 1 May 1991, p. 14.

34. FBIS, 5 February 1991, p. 22.

35. FBIS, 7 November 1990, p. 28.

36. FBIS, 19 October 1990, p. 27-8.

37. Christine Helms, *Iraq: Eastern Flank of the Arab World* (Washington, D.C.: Brookings Institution, 1984).

38. Economist Intelligence Unit, *Quarterly Economic Report on Iraq*, 2 (1992): 1.

39. "Embargo of Iraq Develops Leaks," *Los Angeles Times*, 28 June 1992, A1.

40. Economist Intelligence Unit, *Quarterly Economic Report on Iraq* , 3 (1990): 14.

41. FBIS, 28 April 1992, p. 25. Hassan and the MIO were also key play-

ers in maintaining Iraq's secret biological weapons program.

42. Ibid., 19.

43. FBIS, 11 December 1990, p. 21.

44. Clawson, *How Has Saddam Hussein Survived?* 21.

45. Ibid., 25.

6

The Future of Sanctions

To simply say that economic sanctions do not "work" would not be an addition to the field of international relations. To be of any value, this study must assist policymakers in determining how and why different types of sanctions are effective and why they may be counterproductive. Doing so not only expands our knowledge of how this particular tool of foreign policy can and should be used but also how states can use their economic power to exercise influence in the international environment.

The counterproductive tendencies of export sanctions should not be overstated. When sanctions are imposed with sufficient stringency, they will have an overall wealth-reducing effect on the economy of the target, which could cause enough economic pain to coerce cooperative behavior. However, this outcome is relatively rare. As Hufbauer and Schott note in *Economic Sanctions Reconsidered*, sanctions result in compliance in approximately one-third of the cases they investigated, which leave two-thirds that were at the very least ineffective. But whether or not sanctions were effective in a particular case is not a function of their aggregate wealth-reducing impact on the economy, rather it is a consequence of how the impact is distributed across society. If a country simply lacks the ability to produce the goods that have been screened out by sanctions, then the overall wealth reduction cannot be compensated by import substitution. The same is true if the sanctions include domestically unavailable products with highly inelastic demand curves. Oil is a classic example. If the target lacks the ability to produce petroleum products, it is only a matter of time before stringent sanctions impose an unacceptable cost on the economy.

In this light, Haiti has been cited as a case where sanctions should have had a drastic effect on the economy and coerced some sort of compliance from the Haitian military government. Haiti is, after all, the poorest country in the western hemisphere and is unable to provide for many of its needs, including oil. Given Haiti's inability to engage in ISI, we should expect that the government would have been forced to comply with the demands of the international community within a few weeks or months at the most, yet it remained in power and the democratically elected leader of the country, Aristide, stayed in exile until the summer of 1994. Even so, the contribution of the economic pressure toward the Haitian military government's eventual capitulation is questionable. The Haitian junta only agreed to relinquish power when the threat of invasion was absolutely imminent and U. S. armed forces were actually en route.

Sanctions did not have the desired political effect but not out of any failure to have an economic impact. Much as in Iraq, they had devastating consequences for the majority of residents, but the regime was able to insulate itself from popular discontent through brutal repression. The sanctions were aimed mostly at financial and commercial transactions, especially oil imports. In a country such as Haiti, which has no ability to produce fuel or fuel substitutes, the effects should have been paralyzing and in fact they were. Without fuel, the ability of farmers to get their food to market was severely constrained. At the end of 1993, relief agencies predicted that widespread famine could result from the fuel embargo because not only were farmers unable to transport produce to the cities but also because relief agencies lacked the means to transport food to regions that were running short. In addition, the fuel embargo made it prohibitively expensive for workers to travel even short distances in search of employment. One reporter found that the price of bus transportation had quadrupled since sanctions went into place, making it unprofitable for most workers to go anywhere outside of the extremely local area.[1]

Yet despite these extremely desperate circumstances, the military government of Haiti did not feel compelled to accede to the demands of the international community and return control of the country to its democratically elected leadership. If anything, repression became more intense as the notorious FRAPH units patrolled the urban slums and rural areas where Aristide supporters live, leaving behind a trail of mutilated bodies every night. At the same time, it appears that a small but select group may have benefited from sanctions. As the *Los Angeles Times* observed, "the people who were supposed to be harmed, the rich and their military allies, survived; some even prospered as they traded in black-market fuel."[2] So once again we have a situation where sanctions had a significant economic impact on the target but that economic impact failed to have the desired political effect because the regime was sufficiently insulated from popular pressure. Since some of the Haitian elite benefited from sanctions in the form of profits from black market trading, they had an incentive to see that sanctions remain in place. As far as the military regime was concerned, sanctions were in some ways beneficial to its main constituency.

Elasticity of supply is an important variable as well, but in many situations the products blocked by export sanctions may simply have not been produced previous to sanctions because they were cheaper to import. In this situation, import substitute producers will rise to fill in the gap between supply and demand produced by sanctions and capture rents in the form of consumer surplus. This is obviously wealth reducing in the aggregate, but we must consider the ramifications of this process. First, the process creates a group of producers who owe their increased profits, or very existence, to the presence of sanctions, which provides them with a strong incentive to see that sanctions remain in place. The situation is not very different from what tends to occur when trade-prohibiting tariffs are introduced to protect infant industries. The tariff should theoretically remain in place only long enough for the protected industry to become competitive against imports, but this rarely happens. More often than not, the protected industries become bloated rent seekers who continue to extract rents from consumers by doing everything in their power to ensure that the protective tariff stays in place. Export sanctions are simply an externally imposed distortion, and while those who gain from this distortion cannot directly influence the imposing party, they can influence the target country government to act in their interest by continuing or intensifying the policies that prompted the introduction of sanctions.

This raises an important question: If export sanctions are "good" for some producers in the target country, why should they wait for sanctions? The reason may be simply that these producers are unable to see the opportunities. After all, ISI is a government-sponsored program to develop industries and reduce dependence on the more developed nations that are perceived as predatory exploiters of the less developed world. ISI does not occur because a group of producers pressure the government to adopt such policies, but once they have reaped the benefits from ISI they are reluctant to give them up. Likewise, there is no reason to expect that producers will be able to anticipate the benefits they will receive from sanctions. However, once sanctions are in place and import-competing producers begin to realize gains from them, they will take measures to ensure that they will be able to continue to collect that rent. This conception of rent seeking was perhaps summed up best by C. Fred Bergsten: "Government involvement in the market tends to generate rents, and with them a set of incentives for firms to pursue these rents and the relevant bureaucracies to enlarge them."[3] While sanctions do not constitute "government involvement in the market," they are an analogous distortion that produces rent seeking behavior.

One possible criticism of this line of reasoning is that if rent seekers lobby for policies that benefit them at the expense of society at large, we should expect those from whom rents are extracted to counterbalance these efforts. But as research on rent seeking has shown, societies are apparently willing to endure significant costs. India is perhaps the best example of this: Some estimate the loss that rent seeking imposes on the economy to be on the order of 30% of GNP.[4] The theory of rent seeking holds that rent seekers will spend up to the full amount of the expected benefit to obtain government provided benefits. Clearly, sanctions are not a government provided benefit, but the target country government does have some degree of control over the process. If it refuses to comply or intensifies the objectionable actions, sanctions will probably remain in place, thus providing an incentive for those who gain from sanctions to engage in rent seeking just as if it were a government-provided benefit.

It could also be argued that the rent seeking induced by sanctions would be so debilitating to the economy that it would compel compliance by the target country. But this depends on how much rent seeking was occurring before sanctions were imposed. If there was a tremendous amount prior to sanctions, then whatever occurs under sanctions may actually be an improvement. One implication of Anne Krueger's study of rent seeking in Turkey and India is that, "an import prohibition might be preferable to a non-prohibitive quota if there is competition for licenses under the quota. This follows immediately from the fact that a prohibition would release resources from rent seeking and the excess cost of domestic production might be less than the cost of the rents."[5] Trade-disrupting sanctions are the functional equivalent of a import prohibition and, depending on the level of rent seeking that existed prior to sanctions, they may have a relatively beneficial effect in the aggregate.

Another possible criticism of the theory advanced here is that if sanctions can be construed as beneficial to the target country, we should expect to see countries imposing "sanctions" against themselves. The answer to this point is twofold. First, some countries do exactly that by instating trade-prohibiting tariffs. Taiwan and South

Korea are considered two of the great success stories of export-led industrialization, but both used protective tariffs to build competitive industries. Even so, such a tariff may be politically unpopular, because it diverts consumer surplus to domestic producers.

Sanctions give politicians a means around this dilemma by taking the decision out of their hands, thereby creating a constituency that favors the continuation of sanctions for their financial gain while focusing the wrath of those who lose from sanctions on external enemies. While an unpopular tariff could theoretically weaken a government, the link between the losses from sanctions and the policies of the target government is not always clear to citizens of the target country. Depending on the control a government has over the media, it may be able to twist sanctions to its benefit. In Serbia, for example, extensive state control over the media has allowed the government to project an image of an embattled Serbia fighting for its existence against the combined forces of the West.

By the logic of collective action, groups that gain from sanctions have certain advantages over groups that lose as a result of economic isolation. Gainers from export sanctions are a relatively small group consisting of producers and suppliers of goods made unavailable by sanctions, and their profits come at the expense of a much larger group of consumers. Smallness has distinct advantages in such situations. Not only are small groups inherently easier to coordinate and organize, they can also more easily coerce their members into sharing burdens, thus minimizing the "free rider" problem. In addition, smallness provides greater personal incentives because members receive greater individual returns. [6]

In a large population, the obvious temptation for any individual is to allow committed members to work for benefits that they will not be able to deny to others, regardless of whether or not they assisted in the effort. This is the "free rider" problem. There is no incentive, for example, for the average citizen to lobby for clean air regulations. If committed environmentalists are willing to expend time and money lobbying for expanded air quality controls and they succeed, the individuals who did not assist in the effort cannot be denied the benefits of cleaner air. Small groups are not entirely immune from the free rider problem, but because they have fewer members, the problem is more easily controlled.

Smallness also inherently provides greater returns to individual members. In a small group, whatever benefits are obtained will be shared over a relatively small population of individual participants. In a large group, however, the benefits are spread across many more individuals, which means that the return to each individual member is smaller. Therefore, individual participants in a large group have less of a personal incentive to work toward a goal that benefits all members. The dynamics of collective action give distinct advantages to small groups over large groups. By creating an environment in which small groups of producers and suppliers can collect profits in the form of consumer surplus, export sanctions create a situation that exemplifies these advantages.

This study has focused on negative sanctions because the term "sanctions" usually refers to negative forms of influence, but we can expand the definition to include positive economic inducements. Positive sanctions could take many forms. Financial aid or loans would be the obvious examples, but preferential trade agreements, entry into trade blocs, or technical assistance could also serve as positive forms of influence.

Positive sanctions work in a fundamentally different manner from their negative counterpart and, therefore, have different possible uses. While negative sanctions should have the greatest impact when they are used by a dominant power against a dependent partner, positive sanctions should meet with success more often when used between interdependent parties. Economic interdependence weakens the viability of negative sanctions because they may hurt the imposing party as much or more than the target. When the United States threatened to impose stiff tariffs on imported Japanese luxury cars, for example, it was American dealership owners and employees whose livelihood depended on the sale of these cars that protested the loudest. It is, by definition, impossible to harm the economic interests of an interdependent trading partner without harming the economic interests of some sectors at home, even if the target chooses not to retaliate in kind.

In addition, interdependent states with an ongoing relationship expect to work together in the future. In game theoretic terms, they are playing an iterated game in which the behavior of one party is affected by the behavior of the other in previous rounds. In empirical tests, it has been shown that a strategy of initial cooperation followed by either further cooperation if the other party cooperates or defection if he defects ("tit-for-tat") is the most rewarding overall. This can be applied to the use of sanctions between interdependent parties. If positive sanctions are cooperation and negative sanctions are defection, we should expect that among interdependent parties those that play tit-for-tat will do better than those who chose a different strategy. With this point in mind, it is clear that while positive sanctions should lead to cycles of interdependent actors responding cooperatively, the use of negative sanctions could lead to cycles of mutually destructive defection.

A final issue is the effect that sanctions can have on third parties. The United States has imposed sanctions with extraterritorial aspects on Iran, Libya, and Cuba. That is, the sanctions extend to third-party countries that do business with these countries. Although President Clinton issued waivers for most of these provisions, these sanctions were a major sticking point between the United States and many of our closest European trade and security partners. Given the lessons of the cases explored here, we should ask ourselves if the sanctions are truly worth the serious damage they can cause to our relationships with other countries with which we have far more to gain and lose, both in trade and security cooperation.

This issue as well as the general proliferation of sanctions in the 1990s, has forced many in Congress to reconsider how and when the United States uses economic sanctions. Although each episode is different, there are some clear lessons which emerge from this study, and questions that policymakers should ask before resorting to sanctions.

•**Is there a clear and realistic goal?** The historical record shows that sanctions have been most effective when we had clear, limited goals that the target state could meet. Sanctions, for example, have helped to resolve expropriation issues, and persuade others to cancel purchases and sales of military equipment. In most cases, there was a clear quid pro quo. Broad sweeping goals that threaten a regime's survival, however, are not likely to be achieved. Why should a leader comply with a demand that could seriously threaten the existence of his regime? When forced to choose between political survival and economic deprivation that can usually be mitigated, few governments are likely to give into sanctions. On occasion, broad sanctions may be appropriate to signal resolve and indicate displeasure, but we must balance the often times ephemeral utility derived from sanctions against the concrete counterproductive effects.

•**Are the sanctions carefully targeted?** Sanctions are often said to be a blunt instrument, but they can be sharpened through careful consideration of the goals. The Iran missile proliferation sanctions are a good example of well-targeted sanctions. Designed to prevent Iran from acquiring additional advanced ballistic missile components, these sanctions apply to a small group of Russian suppliers who violated their country's export control laws by shipping missile components to Iran. As a consequence, these companies will be excluded from future cooperative ventures with the US government. It is important to note that these sanctions only apply to the few Russian companies that sold missile related items after Russia put its new export control procedures into place. This gets to the heart of the matter without condemning the Russian government or impeding cooperation on other levels.

•**Does international cooperation exist?** It may not be possible to arrange formal multilateral sanctions in all cases, but informal short-term arrangements can be achieved between major suppliers. There are very few areas in which the United States can impose meaningful unilateral sanctions, but even limited international cooperation in high-tech and financial services can be effective against many countries. For example, Libya's chemical weapons program has been stunted by the cooperation of a few key suppliers.[7] In the rarefied world of sophisticated technology, a little cooperation among potential suppliers can go a very long way.

•**What are the costs of the sanctions?** In many cases, sanctions direct more pain against Americans that their intended targets. Before they were amended, the sanctions imposed against India and Pakistan as a result of their nuclear tests blocked sales of white wheat, which would have done far more damage to the farmers of the Pacific Northwest (where most of that grain is produced) than the intended targets, who would have simply found other suppliers. The key point is the concentration of supply. If the U. S. is one of the few potential suppliers, then sanctions can bite. If we are easily replaced with alternative suppliers at minimal cost, we will harm no one but ourselves.

•**When do sanctions end?** There should always be a trigger for ending sanctions, and if it is not reached within a set timeframe, we should reconsider our methods. Given the potential costs of leaving sanctions in place indefinitely, we must be willing to periodically reassess their utility in specific cases.

While examples of poorly constructed and counterproductive sanctions abound, it is simply not true to state that economic sanctions never work. At the same time, it is clear they have become an overused tool of American foreign policy, as we fling sanctions at every transgression, whatever the consequences might be. By keeping the above points in mind, policy makers will have a better chance of using American economic power to secure foreign policy goals.

The end of the Cold War presents both challenges and opportunities for American foreign policy. Essentially isolationist voices call for the United States to relinquish its role as the predominant power in world affairs and focus on domestic problems, but this view ignores the historical reality that great powers, which fail to counter minor threats, soon find themselves battling much more serious challenges. On the other hand, where the Cold War provided a context for military action across the world, military force is now no longer appropriate or desirable in many circumstances. In a globally interdependent economy, sanctions can play a role in shaping the behavior of states, but we must first understand their effects. By doing so, we expand the range of options available to American policy makers as we confront the security challenges of the twenty-first century.

NOTES

1. "In Sanctions Wake, Haiti's Poor on Verge of Starvation," *Los Angeles Times*, 20 December 1993, A20.

2. Ibid.

3. C. Fred Bergsten and Marcus Noland, *Reconcilable Differences? United States-Japan Economic Conflict* (Washington D.C.: Institute for International Economics, 1993), 61.

4. S. Mohammad and J. Whalley, "Rent Seeking in India," *Kyklos* 37, no. 3 (1984).

5. Anne O. Krueger, "The Political Economy of the Rent Seeking Society" *American Economic Review* 64, no. 3 (1974): 301.

6. Mancur Olson, *The Logic of Collective Action: Public Goods and the Theory of Groups* (Cambridge: Harvard University Press, 1971).

7. "Libya hampered by decade-old ban," *Jane's Defence Weekly*, 12 August 1998, 7.

Appendix I

Notes on Methodology and Cases

To exclude the possibility that the production increases attributed to sanctions are a product of normal growth, each of the cases in the study was paired with a similar country to create a control group of 20 countries that were similar to the cases in the sample, with the notable exception that they had not experienced sanctions.[1]   However, the variables controlled for do not appear to be statistically significant. While growth in manufacturing in the control pairs varies considerably, on average there is only a 12% difference between the before and after rates of growth. This can be taken as an average baseline exponential growth rate, yet the cases in the study greatly exceed the baseline.

AVERAGE GROWTH RATES	
Control Group	12%
Financial Sanctions	36%
Trade-Disrupting Sanctions	246%

There are other factors that could account for the variance in the amount of import substitution industrialization that occurs. First, the level of development could be an important factor. The more industrialized countries should have greater flexibility and diversity in their manufacturing base and therefore be more agile in adapting to the demands prompted by the imposition of sanctions. Second, labor could be a factor. A more educated labor force should be easier to retrain for new industries, thus easing the transition. Lastly, access to capital may also be a factor. Countries with low interest rates should provide the indigenous manufacturing sector with a cheap means of financing an expansion into new types of production. The results of this study, however, suggest that these variables are not particularly important in explaining the variance in the amount of import substitution.

CORRELATION WITH CHANGE IN RATE OF MANUFACTURING GROWTH

Variables	Correlation
Level of Development[2]	.02
Level of Labor Force Education[3]	.03
Cost of Capital[4]	.06

To prove that sanctions caused the growth in manufacturing, we first must prove that there was no significant difference between the control group and the sanctions cases before the imposition of sanctions. This is done with a linear regression analysis, which found no significant difference ($F<1$) between the control and the test groups before sanctions.

We can now move on to a regression which will explore the importance of the sanction-type variable. These tests were done using an effect coding system of either 1, 0, or -1. The control group was assigned a value of -1. EFFECT 1 assigned a value of 0 to the financial sanctions group and 1 to the trade sanctions group, EFFECT 2 assigned a value of 0 to the trade sanctions group, and 1 to the financial sanctions group. The results of the regression reveal that the difference in growth rates after sanctions between the control group and the test population is almost entirely due to the effect of trade sanctions (EFFECT 1).

Equation 1
(Growth Rate After Sanctions) = 10.5(Constant) + 8.48(EFFECT 1)--3.99(EFFECT 2).
Multiple R = .399
Adjusted R squared = .114
Standard Error = 12.77
t = .04

Equation 2
(Growth Rate After Sanctions) = 10.65(constant) + 5.79(EFFECT 1)
Multiple R = .348
adjusted R squared = .164
Standard Error = 12.88
t =.03

These findings are consistent with the predictions of the model. Financial sanctions restrict the normal flow of capital to the target country while export sanctions restrict the flow of goods, thus export sanctions will provide an incentive to provide substitutes for the restricted goods while purely financial sanctions will not. In this manner at least, financial sanctions may in fact tend to have less of a counterproductive effect associated with their use.

Although most models of sanctions are static, this model assumes that sanctions will produce changes in behavior in the target country as sanctions alter incentives to produce. This is essentially a public choice model insofar as it disaggregates the target state and looks at how different groups within the target country should respond to the pressures of different types of sanctions. As Gary Becker, one of the most influential voices in public choice theory states, "all political systems have been subject to pressures from special interest groups that try to use influence to enhance their welfare."[5] Following from Becker and others in the public choice school, we should expect sanctions to achieve the desired change in policy or behavior when the groups that support those same policies are weakened and opposing groups are strengthened.

A public choice approach helps us to understand why the optimal tariff of a small country can be greater than zero.[6] While for the country as a whole the optimal tariff might be zero on any given product, individuals will have different utility functions depending on what determines their income. Based on the Hecksher-Olin model, we can assume that an individual's income is a product of his ownership of different factors. At its most basic level, this model would have three factors: capital, labor, and land. If an individual's income is determined primarily by any particular factor in a manner disproportionate to the factor distribution in the country as a whole, this individual's optimal tariff rate may be greater than zero. Since tariffs are an additional source of income to certain individuals and sectors, changes in the tariff rate will affect people in the country differently depending on their factor ownership. We can conclude then, that (1) the optimal tariff is positive (negative) for people who are relatively poorly (well) endowed in the imported goods intensively used factor, and (2) the greater the difference between the individual and national endowment ratios, the greater the deviation of individually optimal tariff of subsidy rate from free trade policy.

If one accepts that a public choice approach is useful in the study of behavior under sanctions, there are still some unresolved questions. First, assuming that a group that benefits from sanctions will organize and pressure the government for favorable policies, why should they be successful? Second, if they benefit from sanctions, why don't they organize and take action in the absence of sanctions to obtain this benefit? The first question is best answered by collective action theory. These groups will be relatively small and have the benefits of smallness that Olson has elaborated on, but will reap large benefits from sanctions. In Serbia, for example, it is estimated that only 5%-10% of the population benefits from sanctions. Several investigations of the influence of pressure groups on tariff formation have come to similar a conclusion insofar as that geographic concentration and sectoral concentration are critical variables in determining what groups will be successful in seeing their interests represented in government policy. The best combination would appear to be to be relatively deconcentrated sectorally, while being concentrated geographically. This may not be the most effective organizational strategy in every situation. For example, in nineteenth century America, it appears that the more effective groups were not geographically concentrated, whereas in Great Britain, the effective groups were concentrated. Geographic and sectoral concentration are important variables, but which combination will be most effective is a function of the political system that may be more responsive to sectoral or geographic concentration.

As for the second question, there could be any number of reasons why the groups that benefit from sanctions do not organize in the absence of sanctions. In some instances, it is simply because the group in question could not exist without sanctions. The black market in Yugoslavia would evaporate without sanctions. In other instances, the reason may be simply that these producers are unable to see the opportunities. Throughout the developing world, ISI has been a government-sponsored program to develop industries and reduce dependence on the more developed nations that are perceived as predatory exploiters of the less developed world. ISI in most cases does not occur because producers who believe they might benefit from such a program organize and expend resources to pressure the government to adopt such policies, but once they have reaped the benefits from ISI, they are reluctant to give them up.[7] ISI is fundamentally different from tariff policy in that tariffs are created to protect an existing industry, while ISI is a program designed to create an industry. The critical difference is that when considering tariff formulation we must take into consideration that there is already an existing group that can exert pressure on the government, while in the case of ISI, those that stand to benefit may not exist as a coherent group before the policy is implemented. In addition, there is no reason to expect that producers will be able to anticipate the benefits they will receive from sanctions, but once they are in place and ISI producers begin to realize gains, they will take measures to ensure that they will be able to continue to collect that rent. "Government involvement in the market tends to generate rents," writes Fred Bergsten, "and with them a set of incentives for firms to pursue these rents and the relevant bureaucracies to enlarge them."[8] While sanctions do not constitute "government involvement in the market," they are an analogous distortion that produces rent-seeking behavior.

One might criticize this line of reasoning because by the same logic, if rent seekers lobby for policies that benefit them at the expense of society at large, we should expect those from whom rents are extracted to counterbalance these efforts. But as research on rent seeking has shown, societies are apparently willing to endure significant costs. Take, for example, the cost that litigation imposes on American society. Several studies have been conducted on the wealth-reducing effects of an overabundance of lawyers, and while Shakespeare's recommendation is often repeated, law schools are as full as ever and the United States shows no sign of becoming a less litigious society. India is perhaps an even better example of where a tremendous amount of the GNP is lost to rent seeking; some estimate the loss to be on the order of 30% to 45% of GNP.[9] These losses are tolerated and there is no reason to believe that rent seeking caused by sanctions-distorted production should function any differently. Granted the theory of rent seeking holds that rent seekers will spend up to the full amount of the expected benefit to obtain government provided benefits, and clearly sanctions are not a government provided benefit, but the target country government does have some degree of control over the process. If it refuses to comply or intensifies the objectionable actions, sanctions will probably remain in place, thus providing an incentive for those who gain from sanctions to engage in rent seeking just as if it were a government-provided benefit.

NOTES

1. These similar countries were selected along several criteria: First, the time period matched the time period of the case in the study, which should account for boom or bust cycles in the global economy. Second, each pair was from the same geographic region, which would account for regional growth patterns that might confound the results. Third, the regimes were similar in a general sense of democratic or authoritarian. Fourth, the pairs were similar in their level of development based on per capita GNP. Although there is the possibility that this strategy does not control for every conceivable variable, it does control for a number of factors that might otherwise be responsible for the growth in manufacturing experienced in the cases.

2. Based on electrical consumption per capita.

3. Data taken from *UNESCO Statistical Yearbook,* various years. Based on the percentage of total population over age 15 that is literate.

4. The effective rate of interest was calculated using the following formula: $1+ r = (1+i/1+p) - 1$: r = effective interest rate, I = nominal interest rate, p = inflation. The data used here were drawn from various years of the World Bank publication, International Financial Statistics.

5. Gary Becker, "A Theory of Competition Among Pressure Groups for Political Influence," *Quarterly Journal of Economics*: 3, no. 3 (1983): 375.

6. The countries in this study are all small in the sense that they are price-takers on the world market.

7. Latin America is rife with examples, especially the ISI efforts of Chile, Brazil, and Argentina.

8. C. Fred Bergsten and Marcus Noland, *Reconcilable Differences? United States-Japan Economic Conflict* (Washington, D.C.: Institute for International Economics, 1993), 61.

9. S. Mohammad and J. Whalley, "Rent Seeking in India," *Kyklos* 37, no. 3 (1984).

Appendix II

Cases Examined in Chapter 2

DOMINICAN REPUBLIC

In 1960, Dominican Republic dictator Rafael Trujillo formally surrendered control of the country to a democratically elected president, Joaquin Balaguer, but maintained control of the government and security forces. Trujillo's regime had consistently aroused the ire of the United States for its human rights violations and the kidnapping of a Dominican dissident in 1959 from the United States. As a final outrage, Trujillo attempted to have his long-standing enemy and president of Venezuela, Romulo Betancourt, assassinated.

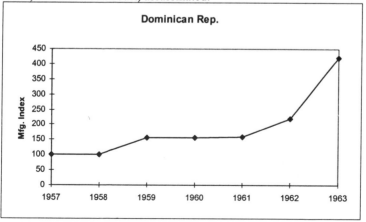

In response to this and the generally brutal oppression existing in the Dominican Republic, the United States along with the Organization of American States (OAS) imposed sanctions, severely limiting the trade of member states with the Dominican Republic. The arms trade was suspended immediately, but sanctions soon included other items such as trucks, electrical equipment, petroleum, and machine parts.

Trujillo was assassinated in May 1961, but his son and the military retained firm control over the country. Human rights violations continued and finally the United States took an active role in supporting Balaguer, sending a naval fleet off Santo Domingo as a show of force. The younger Trujillo was driven into exile, Balaguer set up a provisional government, and the OAS lifted sanctions in January 1963. Sanctions seem to have had a significant impact on the economy and put pressure on an already troubled regime.

SRI LANKA

In January 1961, the socialist government of Sirvamo Bandaranaike created the Ceylon Petroleum Corporation and proceeded to expropriate the assets of U. S. and British oil companies operating in Ceylon (Sri Lanka) valued at approximately $12 million. In 1962, the Ceylon Petroleum Corporation expropriated privately owned service stations and concluded oil deals with the Soviet Union and Romania. In the same year the Hickenlooper amendment, which bars aid to countries that expropriate American property was signed into law. After a

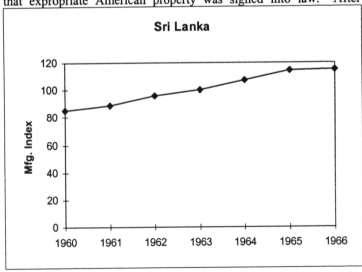

Sri Lanka

series of fruitless negotiations over compensation, the United States suspended all economic aid in February 1963. This made Ceylon's already difficult economic situation even worse and led to a decrease in the popularity of the Bandaranaike government, which attempted to resolve the issue but was unable to do so.

The socialist government finally fell in a March 1965 election to the United National Party (UNP), a conservative party whose main campaign promise was to resolve the expropriation issues and get aid money flowing again. U. S. aid to Ceylon was $17.7 million in 1959, but dropped to $3.9 million in 1963-65, returning to $14 million in 1966. It appears that sanctions in this case were effective in forcing the resolution of the expropriation issue.

BRAZIL

President Janio Quadros resigned after less than a year in office, leaving Brazil in the hands of Vice-President Joao Goulart in September 1961. Goulart was heavily influenced by his brother-in-law and governor of the state of Rio Grande do Sul, Leonel Brizola. Brizola began to expropriate foreign-owned properties in his state worth $135 million, including International Telephone and Telegraph (ITT) assets, and announced that there would be no compensation. In response to these actions, the United States cut economic aid in half for 1962 and 1963.

Goulart attempted to find a middle way between Brizola and the United States which demanded compensation, but was unable to do so without alienating his left-wing support base. The United States indi-

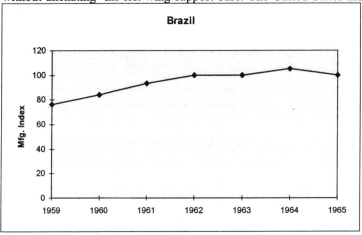

Brazil

cated that it would not automatically condemn militaries in Latin America that overthrow democratically elected governments and prepared to support the Brazilian military with oil shipments in the event of a coup. Goulart continued to issue profit remittance laws and expropriations, which impacted on U. S. interests, but his intervention in internal military affairs proved too much for the Brazilian military. In March 1964, General Castello Branco led a revolt that sent Goulart into exile and began three decades of military rule. Sanctions had some effect in this case by weakening the already weakly supported Goulart government, but the causes of the coup were domestic.

SOUTH AFRICA

As international opposition to the practice of apartheid grew in the early 1960s, sanctions were imposed by the UN against South Africa. The Sharpeville massacre in 1960, in which sixty-four Africans were killed by police, touched off a wave of international opposition to the government's policy of apartheid, which led to South Africa's withdrawal from the Commonwealth. Despite U. S. opposition, in 1962 the UN General Assembly called for all members to break diplomatic relations and impose export and import sanctions. All member states were asked to voluntarily suspend arms sales to South Africa in 1963.

Throughout the 1960s and 1970s, there are more measures taken against South Africa. The United States ceases using South African

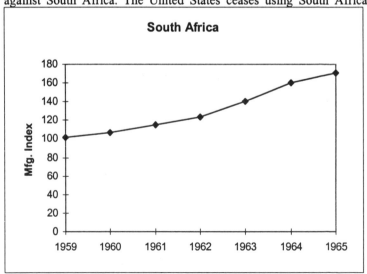

ports for refueling Navy vessels, The International Monetary Fund re-fuses to buy South African gold in excess of $35 per ounce, and South Africa is nearly expelled form the United Nations. After the Soweto riots of 1976, the UN General Assembly approves a resolution to make the arms embargo mandatory. The United States blocks this motion in the Security Council., but the following year takes action to block the sale or re-export of military and police items to South Africa. The arms embargo is significantly strengthened in 1986 by the addition of spare parts and components to list of goods covered by the sanctions.

In the 1990s, South Africa begins to dismantle the apartheid sys-tem and holds multiracial elections leading to the election of President Nelson Mandela. Sanctions had some effect on the reform process. South Africa paid a steep cost for becoming self-sufficient in key in-dustries, and foreign investment slowed considerably throughout the sanctions period.

PORTUGAL

The UN General Assembly voted in 1960 to classify Portugal's Afri-can colonies as "non-self governing " territories, which subjected them to the UN Charter on Decolonization. In the early 1960s, armed rebel-lions broke out in most of Portugal's colonies leading to an Organiza-tion of African Unity resolution calling for a boycott of Portuguese products. The UN General Assembly voted to support the boycott in 1965, but this and other attempts were vetoed by the United

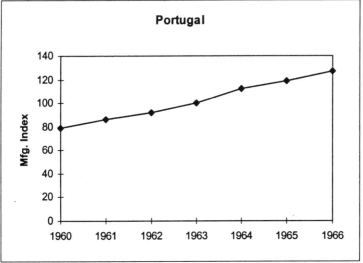

States or Britain in the Security Council. The boycott gained the support of OPEC, which in November of 1973 adopted a resolution cutting off Portugal from Arab oil.

In July 1974, the Portuguese dictatorship fell and decolonization followed rapidly. It is doubtful that the boycott had any real effect on Portugal. The real impetus for the coup was the military's realization that the colonies were indefensible in the face of the growing rebel movements in each of the colonies.

EGYPT

In 1963, Egypt (then known as the United Arab Republic) militarily intervened in Yemen, which aroused some concern in the United States that Egyptian President Nasser may have the destabilization of Saudi Arabia on his agenda. President Kennedy threatened to terminate all U. S. aid including food shipments if the UAR did not remove its troops by the end of 1963. The UAR began to comply in early 1964, but at the same time began to incite anti-American sentiment in the country, leading to several violent incidents against American property and personnel in Egypt.

Nasser later confirmed that Egypt was supporting the rebel forces in the Congo with military and financial assistance. In response, the United States imposed sanctions to pressure the UAR to withdraw from these ventures. The sanctions were mainly a suspension of developmental aid and withholding of PL 480 (food assistance) resources. In October 1965, the U. S. dropped most of the sanctions, but President

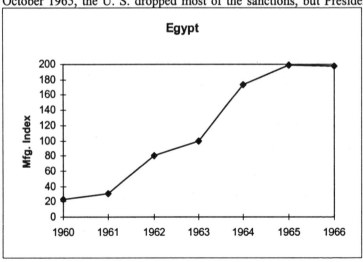

Johnson decided to hold back $37 million worth of PL 480 aid. Throughout 1965, Nasser made several conciliatory moves, including compensation for American property destroyed in 1964 and the appointment of a moderate prime minister. In response, the United States granted Egypt $50 million of PL 480. The sanctions appear to have had some effect on Egypt's actions. While some observers note that it was mainly the failure of Egypt's policies in the Congo that forced its retreat, sanctions made a significant impact on the economy.

INDIA

In 1964, the United States determined that its food aid program was stunting Indian food production, depressing Indian farm prices, and leading to greater dependence on food aid. In an effort to force India to alter its agricultural policy and reduce its dependence on foreign aid, and in order to register displeasure with the India-Pakistan conflict over Kasmir, the United States terminated military aid in August 1965 and suspended food aid programs. India altered its agricultural plan to include the import of high-yield seeds, improved prices for food producers, and increased irrigation. The United States was not yet satisfied and, although it authorized a 1.5 million-ton emergency shipment, long-term agreements were postponed.

In 1966, the new government of Indira Gandhi announced a plan to liberalize import control, attract foreign investment for its fertilizer

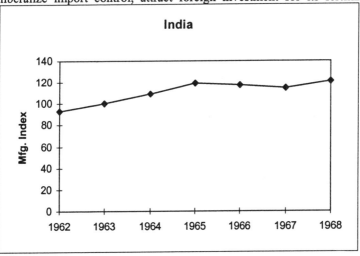

plants, and implement further family planning measures. By the end of 1966, the Indo-Pakistani conflict was settled for the time being and India was making considerable progress toward reducing its dependence on imported food. The United States signed a long-term food aid agreement with India in February 1967. Sanctions clearly had an impact on the Indian government's decisions to accelerate its agricultural reforms and increase production, and India ceased to be plagued by reoccurring famines.

RHODESIA

In 1965, the Rhodesian government issued the Unilateral Declaration of Independence, removing itself from the legislative jurisdiction of the British Government, which was pressuring Rhodesia to begin a transformation to democratic majority rule. White settlers, alarmed by the prospect of relinquishing control of Rhodesia to Black Africans, rallied behind Ian Smith, who promised to maintain white rule. In response, the United Kingdom (UK) imposed stringent sanctions on Rhodesia, which, given that the majority of Rhodesia's trade was conducted with the UK, should have had disastrous effects on the Rhodesian economy.

The UN also called on all members to break economic relations with Rhodesia. Sanctions were strengthened over the next few years, and in 1968, the UN passed a resolution calling for the complete ban of all imports and exports to and from Rhodesia. Several loopholes in the sanctions were subsequently covered in a 1976 Security Council resolution, making these some of the most stringent sanctions ever imposed against any country.

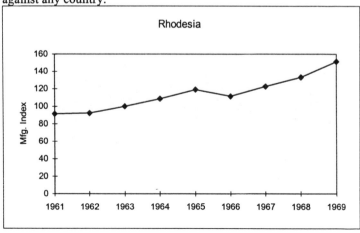

Rhodesia

South Africa provided valuable assistance to Rhodesia from 1965 until 1976, transshipping goods and providing oil. In 1976, however, South Africa imposed sanctions to persuade Smith to accept the Kissinger plan which called for a two-year transition to majority rule. Finally in 1978 Smith offered a settlement which led to free multiracial elections in 1979. While sanctions had some effect, especially at the end, it was the protracted civil war that finally weakened the Smith government.

PERU

Sanctions were imposed by the U. S. against Peru from 1968 to 1974 over the Peruvian government's expropriation of the property and holdings of the International Petroleum Company (IPC), a subsidiary of Standard Oil. The primary economic weapon used was to severely reduce the amount of aid Peru received from the U. S. and international organizations.

Inter-American Development Bank loans were cut severely in 1969 and 1970, and the International Monetary Fund canceled loans for a total of nearly $35 million. In response, Peru expanded its nationalization and expropriation campaign to include agricultural lands owned by American companies, banks, and the ITT telephone system. In 1973, however, Peru agreed to negotiate its expropriation claims and signed an agreement in 1974, which compensated American companies and individuals at approximately market value. Sanctions definitely affected Peru's decision to offer compensation for expropriated property. The reduction in loans affected Peru's credit rating and left it in need of a speedy resolution to the expropriation crisis.

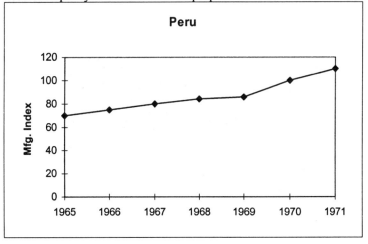

CHILE

Following the election of Salvador Allende in 1970, the United States begins a gradual process of trying to weaken the ability of the Allende government to govern effectively through financial pressure. First the U. S. cut off bilateral aid in November 1970. Over the next year, U. S. banks reduced Chile's line of credit from $219 million to $32 million. In August 1971, the U. S. Export Import Bank deferred a $21 million loan. As part of the socialist program of Allende, U. S.-owned copper mines were nationalized in September 1971, following which the World Bank refused all new loans to Chile. In November 1971, Chile stopped paying off its foreign debt, which led the EXIM Bank to suspend all loan guarantees.

As the Chilean economy went into a tailspin, the military staged a coup in September 1973. It is difficult in the Chilean case to isolate the effect of sanctions because of the covert actions of the U. S., however, most observers agree that it was mainly the ineptitude of the Allende government in handling the economy and the increasing violent activity of the far left that triggered the coup.

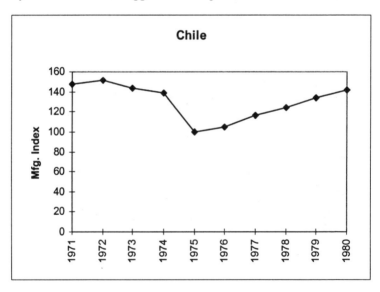

SOUTH KOREA

In 1972, President Park of Korea declared martial law and dissolved the National Assembly. The Korean Central Intelligence Agency (KCIA) kidnapped dissident Kim Dae Jung from Tokyo, which sparked international protests. In response to growing unrest, Park tightened internal security, even further restricting political freedom.

In 1973, the U. S. Congress enacted section 26 of the Foreign Assistance Act, limiting military assistance to Korea until progress was made in reducing human rights violations. The following year Congress reduced military assistance by $20 million dollars. As arrests and torture continued, Congress considered further reductions in aid, but the necessity of insuring South Korea's security against threats from North Korea overrode the human rights concerns. President Carter emphasized human rights in a joint communiqué with South Korean dissidents, but refrained from imposing more stringent sanctions.

By 1981, human rights were conspicuously absent from Korean-American discussions. The sanctions in this case were not effective because the American government was reluctant to link human rights to security assistance.

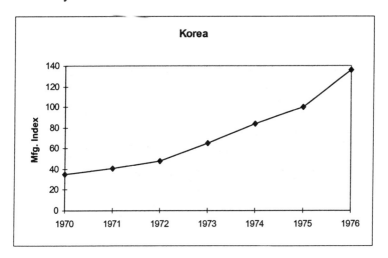

TURKEY

In 1974, Turkey invaded and occupied the northern half of the island of Cyprus. The U. S. Congress immediately voted to cut off all military aid to Turkey, but President Ford postponed the cut off for several months. Immediately before the ban was to go into effect, the U. S. Defense department announced a plan to sell $230 million worth of tank equipment to Turkey. After U. S. military activity from bases in Turkey was severely limited by the Turkish government, Congress voted to allow some sales of military equipment, but prohibited new military assistance grants. In 1976, President Ford announced a plan to sell $125 million in military equipment to Turkey. In 1978, Congress voted to end all restrictions on arms sales to Turkey.

Turkey clearly defeated American attempts to influence its actions in Cyprus. Although the United States was the primary supplier of military equipment to Turkey and should therefore have had some leverage regarding Cyprus, Turkey was able to effectively negate American pressure. Given its strategic location on the southern perimeter of the Soviet Union and the numerous American military bases on Turkish soil, Turkey could exert effective pressure on the United States. This is an example of sanctions between what were effectively two interdependent parties. For reasons explained in Chapter 6, positive inducements could have been more effective in this case.

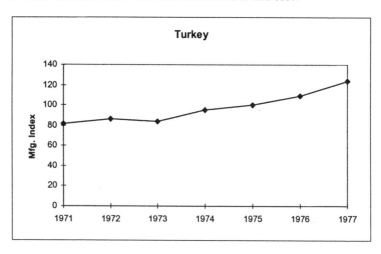

URUGUAY

Sanctions were imposed as a means of persuading the military government to end human rights abuses. In 1975 and 1976, a series of measures were enacted, suspending military and economic aid as well as Inter-American Development Bank support. In October 1976, all military aid was denied, and in February 1977, economic aid was blocked. Finally in July 1977, export of police equipment was denied. Following some indications that human rights violation had decreased, the sanctions were lifted in 1981. Sanctions appear to have had some impact on the behavior of the Uruguayan Junta. Following the suspension of aid, some political prisoners were released and the regime began to prosecute officers believed guilty of the worst abuses.

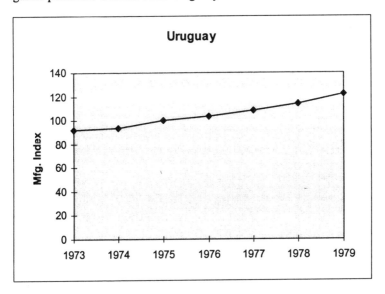

ARGENTINA

In response to human rights violations, the U. S. severely reduced financial and military aid, and blocked the export of U. S. military and police equipment. In February 1977, President Carter announced that aid to Argentina would be reduced to $15 million for fiscal year 1978, down from $36 million the previous year. At the same time, military aid was cut off completely. In July 1977, the U. S. EXIM bank refused a $270 million loan, and the sale of police equipment was barred. In

September 1978, the Department of Defense blocked consideration of 212 license requests for $100 million in military equipment. Following some indication that the condition of human rights had improved in Argentina, the U. S. Senate voted to repeal the ban on military sales.

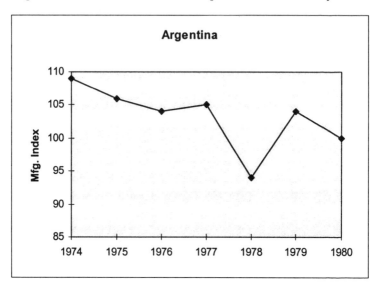

Argentina

EGYPT, 1978

In 1978, Egypt signed the Camp David Accords with Israel, thereby breaking formally with the rest of the Arab world in recognizing the state of Israel. The Arab League, with the exception of Morocco, Sudan, and Oman, threatened to impose a complete boycott on trade and aid with Egypt beginning in March 1978. In response, the U. S. offered $4.8 billion in additional aid to Egypt. The Arab League implemented somewhat less stringent sanctions, and at Saudi Arabia's request, did not take retaliatory measures against the U. S. By December 1983, however, Jordan agreed to resume trade with Egypt. Saudi Arabia and other Gulf states soon followed and trade resumed between Egypt and most other Arab states. Sanctions failed in this case because by agreeing to the Camp David Accords, Egypt gained a huge amount of American financial support, which offset the losses in trade and aid from the rest of the Arab world. The Arab League's influence over Egypt's actions was limited because the United States essentially agreed to absorb the financial cost of incurring the wrath of the Arab states.

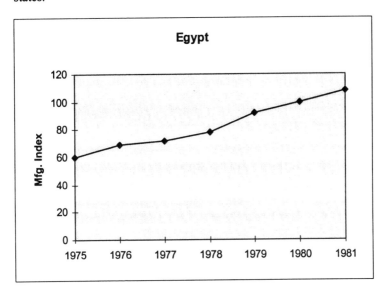

Egypt

BOLIVIA

In response to a military coup, human rights violations and allegations that the Bolivian military was involved in the Andean drug trade, the U. S. suspended all economic and military aid to Bolivia for the 1980 fiscal year. Aid was promised to resume following the resignation of the leader of the military government, General Alberto Natusch Busch, and the installation of a civilian president in November 1979. However, the military staged another coup in July 1980, prompting the U. S. to withdraw its ambassador, suspend aid, and cancel military training.

The Reagan administration decided to maintain the sanctions because of Bolivia's continuing lack of cooperation with the Drug Enforcement Agency. In 1982, a civilian government was installed and aid resumed. The suspension of economic assistance magnified the troubles of the Bolivian economy, which prompted General Natusch to step down in 1980. The maintenance of the financial sanctions also caused a run on the Bolivian peso and led to the fall of the other two military governments.

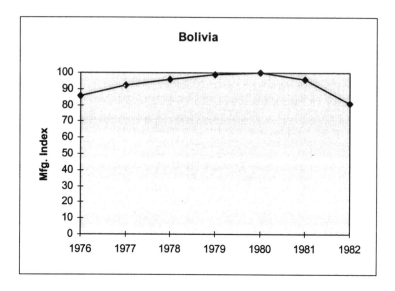

IRAN

In the wake of the Iranian Revolution of 1979, the U. S. Embassy was seized by Islamic radicals in November 1979. The Carter Administration responded first by attempting to negotiate the release of the hostages, but Iranian officials refused to receive American emissaries.

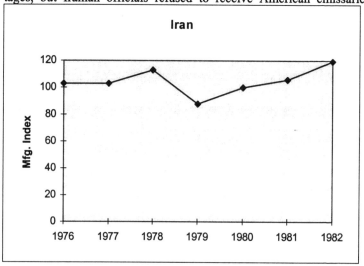

Invoking the International Emergency Economic Powers Act, Carter froze Iranian deposits in U. S. banks. A few days later Iran released some of the hostages but kept most. In February 1980, the U. S. announced that additional sanctions would not be imposed immediately while diplomatic negotiations continued, but in April, Carter announced more stringent sanctions. The new measures included a complete embargo on American exports to Iran, excluding food and medicine; the closure of the Iranian embassy; and the prohibition of financial transactions between American and Iranian citizens. The hostages were finally released in January 1981 following the inauguration of Ronald Reagan. Sanctions appear to have had little effect on the actions of the Iranian government.

TURKEY, 1980

In September 1980, the Turkish military took control of the government, suspending democratic processes. The member countries of the OECD agreed to cut aid to Turkey and the European Trade Union Confederation urged the European Community (EC) to suspend all trade with Turkey. While this did not occur, the EC does suspend a $500 million aid package, and Germany withheld $200 million in aid. After the former Turkish Prime Minister is sentenced to prison, the EC suspended an additional $500 million in aid and the European Parliament voted to end its links with Turkish parliamentarians. Despite the

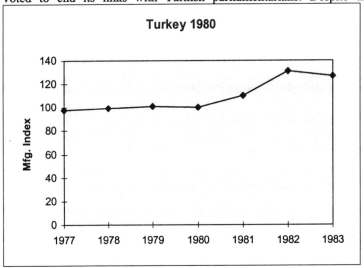

Turkey 1980

obvious hostility of the EC to the military regime, the Turkish Foreign Minister announced Turkey's intent to apply for full membership in the EC.

By 1982, however, the Turkish military had taken steps to return the country to civilian rule, and in 1983 legalized the formation of political parties and set a date for parliamentary elections. Aid resumed the same year. Sanctions played a role in the redemocratization of Turkey because not only was it in need of European aid, it also desired to join the EC at some point in the future and realized that this would be impossible as long as the country was under military rule.

POLAND

In an attempt to break the growing power of the Solidarity union movement, the Polish government imposed martial law in December 1981. The U. S. responded with sanctions that ended Export-Import Bank credit insurance, denied landing rights to Polish airlines, restricted high-tech sales, and later suspended Poland's Most Favored Nation (MFN) status. Following the lifting of martial law and the release of significant numbers of political prisoners, the U. S. gradually lifted sanctions in late 1984.

On balance, it appears that sanctions had some effect on the Polish government. The revocation of MFN status cost Poland tens of millions

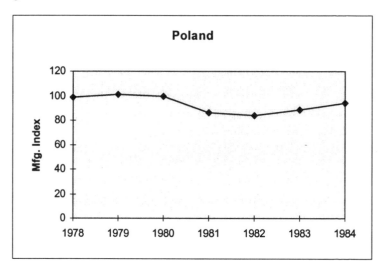

of dollars per year, and the denial of landing and fishing rights was a blow to the economy as well. The denial of credits for food purchases was also damaging and led to increased shortages. While sanctions did not lead to complete liberalization, they did help win the release of some political prisoners and speed the end of formal martial law.

SYRIA

In 1977, Senator Abraham Ribcoff introduced the Omnibus Antiterrorism Act of 1977, which allowed Congress to add countries to a list of suspected terrorist supporting states. Syria, along with Yemen, Iraq, and Libya, was put on the list in late 1980 after the U. S. State Department declared it has repeatedly provided support for terrorist groups. Under the terms of the Ribcoff act and subsequent congressional acts, Syria was denied a variety of American financial aid programs, and serious export restrictions were imposed. Syria eventually reduced some of its more open support for terrorist groups, but it is unclear how much of this moderation was owed to sanctions.

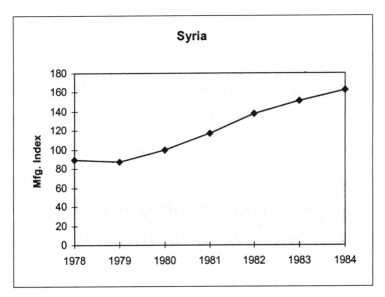

Bibliography

Anglin, Douglas. "United Nations Economic Sanctions Against Rhodesia and South Africa." In *The Utility of Economic Sanctions*, Edited by David Leyton-Brown. London: Croom-Helm, 1985.

Armstrong, Adrianne. "The Political Consequences of Economic Dependence." *Journal of Conflict Resolution* 25, no. 3 (1981): 401-28.

Aspin, Les. *The Aspin Papers: Sanctions Diplomacy and War in the Persian Gulf*. Washington, D.C.: The Center for Strategic and International Studies, 1991.

Bailey, Cheryl Schoenhardt. *A Model of Trade Policy Liberalization looking inside the British Hegemon*, Ph.D. diss. (University of California Los Angeles, 1991).

Baldwin, David. *America in an Interdependent World*. Hanover: University Press of New England, 1976.

_____. *Economic Statecraft*. Princeton: Princeton University Press, 1985.

_____. "The Power of Positive Sanctions." *World Politics* 24, no. 1 (1971): 19-38.

Baring, Alexander. *An Inquiry into the Causes and Consequences of the Orders in Council: and an Examination of the Conduct of Great Britain towards the Neutral Commerce of America*. London, 1808.

Becker, C. M. "Economic Sanctions Against South Africa." *World Politics* 39, no. 2 (1987): 147-73.

Becker, Gary. "A Theory of Competition Among Pressure Groups for Political Influence." *Quarterly Journal of Economics* 98, no. 3 (1983).

Bhagwati, J. "Lobbying and Welfare." *Journal of Public Economics* 14, no. 2 (1980): 355-63.

Bhagwati, J. and N. Ramaswami. "Domestic Distortions, Tariffs and the Theory of Optimal Subsidy." *Journal of Political Economy* 71, no. 1 (1963): 44-50.

Bhagwati, J. and T. N. Srinivasan, "Revenue Seeking: A Generalization of the Theory of Tariffs." *Journal of Political Economy* 88, no. 4 (1980): 1069-87.

Black, P. A. "Economic Sanctions, Monopoly and X-Inefficiency." *South African Journal of Economics* 59, no. 4 (1990): 455-74.

Black, P. A. and J. H. Cooper. "Economic Sanctions and Interest Group Analysis--Some Reservations." *South African Journal of Economics* 57, no. 2 (1989): 385-404.

Blau, Peter. *Exchange and Power in Social Life*. New York: John Wiley, 1964.

Bowman, Larry W. "Organization, Power and Decision-making Within the Rhodesian Front." *Journal of Commonwealth Studies* 7, no. 2 (1969): 145-65.

Brock, William and Stephan Magee. "The Economics of Special Interest Politics: The Case of the Tariff." *American Economic Review* 68, no. 2 (1978): 246-50.

Browning, Edgar. "On the Welfare Cost of Transfers." *Kyklos* 26, no. 2 (1974): 374-77.

Brunn, Geoffrey. *Europe and the French Imperium*. New York: Harper and Row, 1938.

Buchanan, R., R. Tollison and G. Tullock. *Toward a Theory of the Rent Seeking Society*. College Station: Texas A&M University Press, 1980.

Caves, Richard. "Economic Models of Political Choice: Canada's Tariff Structure." *Canadian Journal of Economics* 9, no. 2 (1976): 278-300.

Cifry, M. and C. Cerf, eds. *The Gulf War Reader*. New York: Random House, 1991.

Clark, Evans, ed. *Boycotts and Peace. A Report by the Commission on Economic Sanctions*. New York: Harper and Row, 1932.

Clawson, Patrick. *How Has Saddam Hussein Survived? Economic Sanctions, 1990-1993*. Institute for National Strategic Studies, National Defense University, McNair Paper 22. September 1993.

Cockton, Peter, ed. *House of Commons Parliamentary Papers 1801-1900* Vol. 10. Cambridge: Chadwick-Healey, 1987.

Cohen, Lenard. *Regime Transformation in a Disintegrating Yugoslavia: The Law of Rule vs. the Rule of Law*. The Carl Beck Papers in

Russian and Eastern European Studies, University of Pittsburgh Center for Russian and Eastern European Studies No. 908. 1992.

Cooper, J. H. "On Income Distribution and Economic Sanctions." *South African Journal of Economics* 57, no. 1 (1989): 14-21.

_____. "Sanctions and Economic Theory." *South African Journal of Economics* 53, no. 3 (1985): 287-96.

Cowling, K. and D. Mueller. "The Social Costs of Monopoly Power." *Economic Journal* 88, no. 4 (1978): 727-48.

Crain, Mark. "On The Structure and Stability of Political Markets." *Journal of Political Economy* 85, no. 3 (1977): 829-42.

Curtin, T. and D. Murray. *Economic Sanctions and Rhodesia*. London: Institute of International Affairs, 1967.

_____. "Total Sanctions and Economic Development in Rhodesia." *Journal of Commonwealth Studies* 7, no. 2 (1969): 126-31.

Deutsch, Karl and William Foltz, eds. *Nation-Building*. New York: Atherton Press, 1963.

Dollery, B. E. "Apartheid and the Case for Sanctions." *Journal of Commonwealth and Comparative Politics* 26, no. 3 (1988): 338-40.

Doxey, M. *Economic Sanctions and Problems of International Enforcement*. London: Oxford University Press, 1971.

_____. "International Sanctions: A Framework for Analysis with Special Reference to the UN and South Africa." *International Organization* 26, no. 3 (1972): 527-50.

Economist Intelligence Unit, *Quarterly Economic Review of Ceylon* 41 (March 1963).

_____. *Quarterly Economic Review of Ceylon* 42 (May 1963).

_____. *Quarterly Economic Review of Ceylon* 45 (March 1964).

_____. *Quarterly Economic Review of Ceylon* 48 (November 1964).

_____. *Quarterly Economic Review of Rhodesia, Zambia, and Malawi* 52 (December 1965).

_____. *Quarterly Economic Review of Rhodesia, Zambia, and Malawi* 53 (February 1966).

_____. *Quarterly Economic Review of Rhodesia, Zambia, and Malawi* 54 (May 1966).

_____. *Quarterly Economic Review of Rhodesia, Zambia, and Malawi* 55 (August 1966).

_____. *Quarterly Economic Report on Iraq* 2 (1992).

_____. *Quarterly Economic Report on Iraq* 3 (1990).

_____. *Quarterly Economic Report on Iraq* 4 (1990).

Eden, Frederick. *Eight Letters on the Peace and on the Commerce and Manufactures of Great Britain*. London: 1802.

Ekelund, Robert, and Robert Tollison. *Mercantilism as a Rent Seeking Society: Economic Regulation in Historical Perspective.* College Station: Tex. A&M University Press, 1982.

Elliot, Kimberly Ann. "Sanctions Will Work, and Soon." *New York Times*, 3 August 1990, A27.

Foster, Edward. "The Treatment of Rents in Cost-Benefit Analysis." *American Economic Review* 71, no. 2 (1981): 171-78.

Frankel, Jeffrey. "The 1808-1809 Embargo of Britain." *Journal of Economic History* 42, no. 2 (1982) : 291-302.

Galtung, Johan. "On The Effect of International Economic Sanctions." *World Politics.* 19, no. 3 (1967): 378-416.

Gayer, A., W. Rostow, and A. Swartz. *The Growth and Fluctuation of the British Economy 1790-1850.* Vol. 1. London: Barnes and Noble, 1953.

Gorvin, Ian, ed. *Elections Since 1945.* Chicago: St. James Press, 1989.

Grieve, Muriel. "Economic Sanctions: Theory and Practice." *International Relations* 3, no. 6 (1968): 431-44.

Hansard, T. C. *The Parliamentary Debates from the Year 1803 to the Present Time.* London: Longman Hurst, 1812.

Harberger, Arnold. "Monopoly and Resource Allocation." *American Economic Review* 44, no. 2 (1954): 77-87.

Hecksher, Eli. *The Continental System: An Economic Interpretation.* Oxford: Clarendon Press, 1922.

Helms, Christine. *Iraq: Eastern Flank of the Arab World.* Washington, D.C.: Brookings Institution, 1984.

Hufbauer, Gary and Kimberly Elliott. "Sanctions will Bite and Soon." *New York Times*, 14 January 1991, A17.

Hufbauer, Gary, J. Schott, and K. Elliot. *Economic Sanctions Reconsidered.* Washington, D.C.: Institute for International Economics, 1985.

Kaempfer, W. and A. Lowenberg. "Determinants of the Economic and Political Effects of Trade Sanctions." *South African Journal of Economics* 56, no. 4 (1988): 270-77.

_____. "Economic Sanctions and Interest Group Analysis- A Reply." *South African Journal of Economics.* 59, no. 1 (1991): 92-97.

_____. *International Economic Sanctions* Boulder, CO.: Westview Press , 1992.

Kelidar, Abbas, ed. *The Integration of Modern Iraq.* London: Croom-Helm, 1979.

Keohane, R. and J. Nye. *Power and Interdependence.* Boston: Little, Brown and Company, 1977.

Kippis, Andrew. *Considerations on the Provisional Treaty with America.* London, 1783.

Klein, Burton. *Germany's Economic Preparations for War*. Cambridge: Harvard University Press, 1959.

Knorr, Klaus and F. Trager, eds. *Economic Issues and National Security*. Lawrence: University of Kansas Press, 1982.

Krueger, Anne. "The Political Economy of the Rent Seeking Society" *American Economic Review* 64, no. 3 (1974): 291-303.

Lasswell, H. and A. Kaplan. *Power and Society* Cambridge: Harvard University Press, 1950.

Leidy, M. P. "The Theory of International Economic Sanctions--A Public Choice Approach." *American Economic Review* 79, no. 5 (1989): 1300-3.

Lenway, Stepahnie Ann. "Between War and Commerce: Economic Sanctions as a Tool of Statecraft." *International Organization* 42, no. 2 (1988): 397-426.

Linsay, J. M. "Trade Sanctions as Policy Instruments: A Re-examination." *International Studies Quarterly* 30, no. 2 (1986): 153-74.

Love, J. "The Potential Impact of Economic Sanctions Against South Africa." *Journal of Modern African Studies* 64, no. 2 (1988): 91-111.

Lundborg, Per. *The Economics of Export Embargoes: The Case of U.S.-Soviet Grain Suspension* London: Croom-Helm, 1987.

Malan, T. "Economic Sanctions as a Policy Instrument to Effect Change- the Case of South Africa." *Finance and Trade Review* 14 no. 3 (1981): 87-116.

Mann, A. *Mr. Mann's Letter to the Merchants, Manufacturers, and Others, Interested in the Trade to the United States of America*. London, 1808.

Martin, Lisa. *Coercive Cooperation*. Princeton: Princeton University Press, 1991.

McKinnell, R. T. "Economic Sanctions and the Rhodesian Economy." *Journal of Modern African Studies* 7, no. 4 (1969): 559-82.

McWilliams, James P. *ARMSCOR: South Africa's Arms Merchant*. London: Brassey's Press, 1989.

Meirer, Gerald. *International Economics*. New York: Oxford University Press, 1980.

Miller, J. "When Sanctions Worked." *Foreign Policy* 39, no. 3 (1980): 118-29.

Nincic M. and P. Wallersteen, eds. *Dilemmas of Economic Coercion: Sanctions in World Politics*. New York: Praeger Publishers, 1983.

Olson, Richard. "Expropriation and International Economic Coercion: Ceylon and the West 1961-65." *Journal of Developing Areas* 11, no. 2 (1977): 205-26.

Overy, Richard. *The Road to War*. London: BBC Books, 1989.

Parsons, Talcott. "On the Concept of Political Power." *Proceedings of the American Philosophical Society* (June 1963).

Pincus, Jonathan. "Pressure Groups and the Pattern of Tariffs." *Journal of Political Economy* 83, no. 4 (1975): 757-78.

Porter, Richard. "International Trade and Investment Sanctions: Potential Impact on the South African Economy." *Journal of Conflict Resolution* 23, no. 4 (1979): 579-612.

Ramet, Pedro. *Nationalism and Federalism in Yugoslavia, 1963-1983*. Bloomington: Indiana University Press, 1984.

Renwick, Robin. *Economic Sanctions*. Cambridge: Harvard University Center for International Affairs, 1981.

Rosecrance, Richard. "Reward, Punishment and Interdependence." *Journal of Conflict Resolution* 25, no. 1(1981): 31-48.

Rowe, David. *The Domestic Political Economy of International Economic Sanctions*. Center for International Affairs Working Paper No. 93-1 (Harvard University, 1993).

Rowland, Peter. *David Lloyd George: A Biography*. New York: Macmillan Press, 1975.

Schelling, Thomas. *The Strategy of Conflict*. Cambridge: Harvard University Press, 1960.

Schlesinger, Arthur Jr. "White Slave in the Persian Gulf." *The Wall Street Journal*. 7 January 1991, A11.

Smeets, M. "Economic Sanctions Against Iraq--The Ideal Case." *Journal of World Trade* 24, no. 6 (1990).

Snyder G. and P. Diesing. *Conflict Among Nations*. Princeton: Princeton University Press, 1977.

Statistical Office of the United Nations, *Yearbook of Industrial Statistics: Growth in World Industry*. New York: United Nations, 1965-1985.

Stephen, James. *War in Disguise: or, Frauds of the Neutral Flags.* London, 1805.

Stolper, W. F. and P. Samuelson, "Protection and Real Wages." *Review of Economic Studies* 9, no.1 (1941): 58-73.

Strack, Harry. *Rhodesia: The Case of Sanctions*. Lincoln: University of Nebraska Press, 1976.

Sutcliffe, R. B. "The Political Economy of Economic Sanctions." *Journal of Commonwealth Studies* 7, no. 2 (1969): 113-25.

Tollinson, Robert. "Rent Seeking: A Survey." *Kyklos* 35, no. 4 (1982): 575-602.

Tsebelis, George. "Are Sanctions Effective?: A Game Theoretic Analysis." *Journal of Conflict Resolution* 34, no. 1 (1990): 3-28.

United Nations. *Yearbook of International Trade Statistics Statistical Office of the United Nations*. New York, 1960-1984.

United States General Accounting Office. *Report to the Chairman, Committee on Foreign Relations, U.S. Senate, Economic Sanctions: Effectiveness as Tools of Foreign Policy*. Washington, D.C., February 1992.

United States General Accounting Office. *Report to Congressional Requesters: South Africa, Trends in Trade, Lending, and Investment*. Washington, D.C., April 1988.

U. S. House of Representatives, Committee on Armed Services. *The Role of Sanctions in Securing U. S. Interests in the Persian Gulf*. Washington, D.C., December 21, 1990.

Vanbergeijk, P. A. "Success and Failure of Economic Sanctions." *Kyklos* 42, no. 3 (1989): 385-404.

Vernon, Raymond, ed. *The Oil Crisis*. New York: Norton Press, 1976.

Weber, Max. *The Theory of Social and Economic Organization*. New York: Oxford University Press, 1947.

Willett T. and M. Jalaighajar. "U. S. Trade Policy and National Security." *Cato Journal* 3, no. 3 (1983): 717-28.

Williams, Judith Blow. *British Commercial Policy and Trade Expansion 1785-1850*. Oxford: Clarendon Press, 1972.

World Bank. *International Financial Statistics*. New York: World Bank, 1965-1990.

INTERVIEWS

Mihaljo Avramovic, Chief of Staff, Serbian Ministry of the Economy, Belgrade, Yugoslavia, August 15, 1994.

Dr. Jurij Bajec, Director, Belgrade Economics Institute, Belgrade, Yugoslavia, August 12, 1994.

Vesna Ilic, Foreign Press Officer, Ministry of Information of the Republic of Serbia, Belgrade, Yugoslavia, August 8, 1994.

Zarko Korac, Vice-President, Civic Alliance of Serbia, Belgrade, Yugoslavia, August 24, 1994.

Dr. Mirolub Labus, Vice-President of the Democratic Party of Serbia, August 16, 1994.

Harvey Lee, Economic Officer, United States Embassy, Belgrade, Yugoslavia, August 9,1994.

Vladimir Matic, Former Foreign Minister of the Federal Republic of Yugoslavia, May 18, 1994.

Dr. Predrag Simic, Director, Institute of International Politics and Economics, Belgrade Yugoslavia, August 10, 1994.

ARCHIVES

Abstract of the Answers and Returns Made pursuant to An Act for Taking an Account of the Population of Great Britain and of the Increse or Diminution thereof. London: House of Commons, 1812.

Federal Broadcast Information Service, Middle East Report Series, 1990-1993.

Federal Statistics Office, *Basic Socio-Economic Indicators*. Belgrade, Yugoslavia, 1993.

Federal Statistics Office, *Official Election Statistics*. Belgrade, Yugoslavia, 1993.

Index

Intercourse Act, 49, 52-53;
Orders in Council, 42-50, 53-
57, 60-61; shipping, 14, 42,
45-48, 55-56; Stephen,
James, 48; trade with United
States, 51-52; West Indies,
46-47
Gulf War, 2, 9-10, 85, 87, 89, 93-
94

Haiti, 2-3, 81, 102-03
Hecksher-Olin model, 113
Hussein, Saddam, 3, 85, 87-89,
92-93, 96-97

Import controls, 5, 31, 36
Import prohibition, 104
Import sanctions, 4, 9, 13, 22-24,
26, 44, 46, 85-86, 120
Import substitution industrialization, 4, 17-19, 34, 66, 111
Industrial development, 8, 94
India, 104, 108, 115, 123
International cooperation, 5, 7-8,
32, 85-87, 97, 108
Iran, 18-19, 86, 107, 132
Iraq: arable land, 91-92; agricul-
ture, 91-92; Baath Party, 90,
94; dinar, 91, 96; export
earnings, 85-86, 88; Food
and Agricultural Organiza-
tion, 93; food production, 91,
93; industry, 86, 88, 93-94,
103; international coopera-
tion, 85-87, 97; oil production, 87-88; Military Indus-
trialization Organization, 94;
Ministry of Agriculture, 91;
Ministry of Industry and
Military Industrialization, 94;
Revolutionary Command
Council, 90; smuggling, 86;
wheat harvest, 90
Isolationism, 1, 3
League of Nations, 7, 9
Libya, 3, 107-08, 135

Lloyd George, David, 7

Megarian Decree, 6
Mercantilism, 13-14, 41, 44
Milosevic, Slobodan, 66, 68, 72-
74, 76-77, 81

Napoleon, 3, 13-14, 41, 44-47,
52-53
Nationalization of property: Chile,
126; Peru, 125; Sri Lanka,
118

Oil embargo, 79, 97
Oil shocks, 9
Optimal tariff, 113
Orders in Council, 42-46, 48-50,
53-57, 60-61

Peru, 125
Poland, 134
Portugal, 121
Positive sanctions, 106
Protective tariff, 4, 13, 15, 66,
103, 105

Rally Around the Flag Effect, 4, 6,
20-22, 31, 36-38
Rent seeking, 66, 104, 115
Rhodesia: black population, 32;
civil war, 35, 125; elections,
125; exports, 5, 31; immigration, 33; import controls,
5, 31; import substitution, 32,
35; relations with United
Kingdom, 31, 125; Rhode-
sian Front, 31, 34; Smith,
Ian, 31, 35; Unilateral Declaration of Independence, 31,
81, 124

Somalia, 2
South Africa: apartheid, 23-24,
28-31, 120; arms embargo,
28, 121; ARMSCOR, 27-29;
elections, 30; Munitions pro-

About the Author

ZACHARY SELDEN is Research Director for Emerging Threats at Business Executives for National Security, where he focuses on controlling the spread of weapons of mass destruction. He is the coauthor of *Foreign Policy Failure in the White House: Reappraising the Fall of the Shah and the Iran–Contra Affair* (1993).

ISBN 0-275-96387-X

90000>

EAN

9 780275 963873

HARDCOVER BAR CODE